Adults with challenging behaviours perplex and fascinate professionals and services. Often, we don't really understand how to help the person. We miss the distress in their eyes and lives because it is too painful to acknowledge. Even with more modern terms and concepts, we still try to fix the person.

Our approach is an attempt to place the person and their distress at the centre of our efforts, to understand what is the reason (internal or external) for the many reactions, to aid the person work with us to find out what type of citizen they want to be and then help them become that person in their own very individual way.

Please take the time to join us on this journey to help people with challenging behaviours become a part of our society in a real and honourable way.

Online material is available on our website www.civitasvera.org.

Thank you.

Anna Eliatamby
(On behalf of Civitas Vera)

FROM CHALLENGING BEHAVIOURS

TO DISTRESS FACTORS AND REACTIONS

ANNA ELIATAMBY

Previously published as "From Challenging Behaviours to
Distress Factors and Reactions" by Civitas Vera.

Anna Eliatamby
Suite 179, 226 High Street, Croydon CR9 1DF
Email: civitasvera@gmail.com
Web: www.civitasvera.org

ISBN: 978-1-912680-52-8 (Paperback)
ISBN: 978-1-912680-53-5 (Ebook)

British Library Cataloguing in Publication Data.
A catalogue record for this book is available from the British Library.

Dedication and inspiration

This book is dedicated to the people who taught us: Lisa, Timmy, Phyllis and Iris, Michael and David, Maria, EJ and Zoe. We hope we helped them a little. Thanks are also due to John Hattersley, Catherine Dooley, Roger Blunden and Glynis Murphy who helped us learn how to apply what we acquired in a human way. They all have been and are strong advocates of being value-based and caring and taught us many things, including the importance of strength of character.

Some of the inspiration for how we have worked also comes from learning from Herb Lovett who, sadly, is no longer with us. He was so far ahead of his time and taught us many things. We are also indebted to Tony Carr for his vision for us.

Thanks are also due to Kerri for her input, Damith Jayasinghe for the artwork, Karen Hobden for professional typesetting and Jo Hathaway for editing and advice. All the work done was excellent.

Thank you.

Contents

Foreword

Professional training has often significantly informed the mental, psychological, and emotional frameworks within which we, as professional people and carers, operate when we work with adults with challenging behaviours (people who are also sometimes described as 'people who challenge'). These mindsets are often very clinical, removed from the humanity, emotion, and distress of the situation: these aspects are rarely properly discussed. Because of the distress involved, we tend to distance ourselves from the humanity of the situation and focus on the behaviour, often as something to be removed if possible.

This book is an attempt to move our mindsets away from this to seeing and acknowledging the humanity and the distress of the situation for the person and the people in their life. The focus is on supporting adults.

We use the terms 'distress factors and reactions' instead of challenging behaviours. We consider that it is a more realistic description that conveys the sadness and the emotion that is often so much a part of the person's life, and an acknowledgement that we don't often pay attention to the feelings accompanying the behaviours.

Our approach is an attempt to humanise the situation so that we really pay attention to and focus on the important issues so that the person can have the life they deserve and want. We begin by describing the terms; we then go on to provide you with some questions so that you can decide whether help is needed around the reactions of concern, or in fact if it is not—because we often jump in too easily to aid the person rather than support them to help themselves.

We offer a methodology to look at the person's life and arrive at a range of solutions for the person and others in their life. Each chapter starts with a letter you can use to explain the process. We have included some case studies to help you better understand our approach. These case studies and stories are fictional and not based on specific people we have supported. The aim is to help us think more deeply about the impact we have on the lives of others.

The appendices contain some supplemental questions and information about people and their differences, e.g. autism, depression, happiness, and wellbeing, as well as information on systems-oriented factors, e.g. the psychology of respect, building collaboration in teams.

We have done our best to make it as practical as possible; we hope you will find it an easy-to-use and effective resource. Thank you.

Anna Eliatamby

Chapter One

WHAT ARE DISTRESS FACTORS AND REACTIONS?

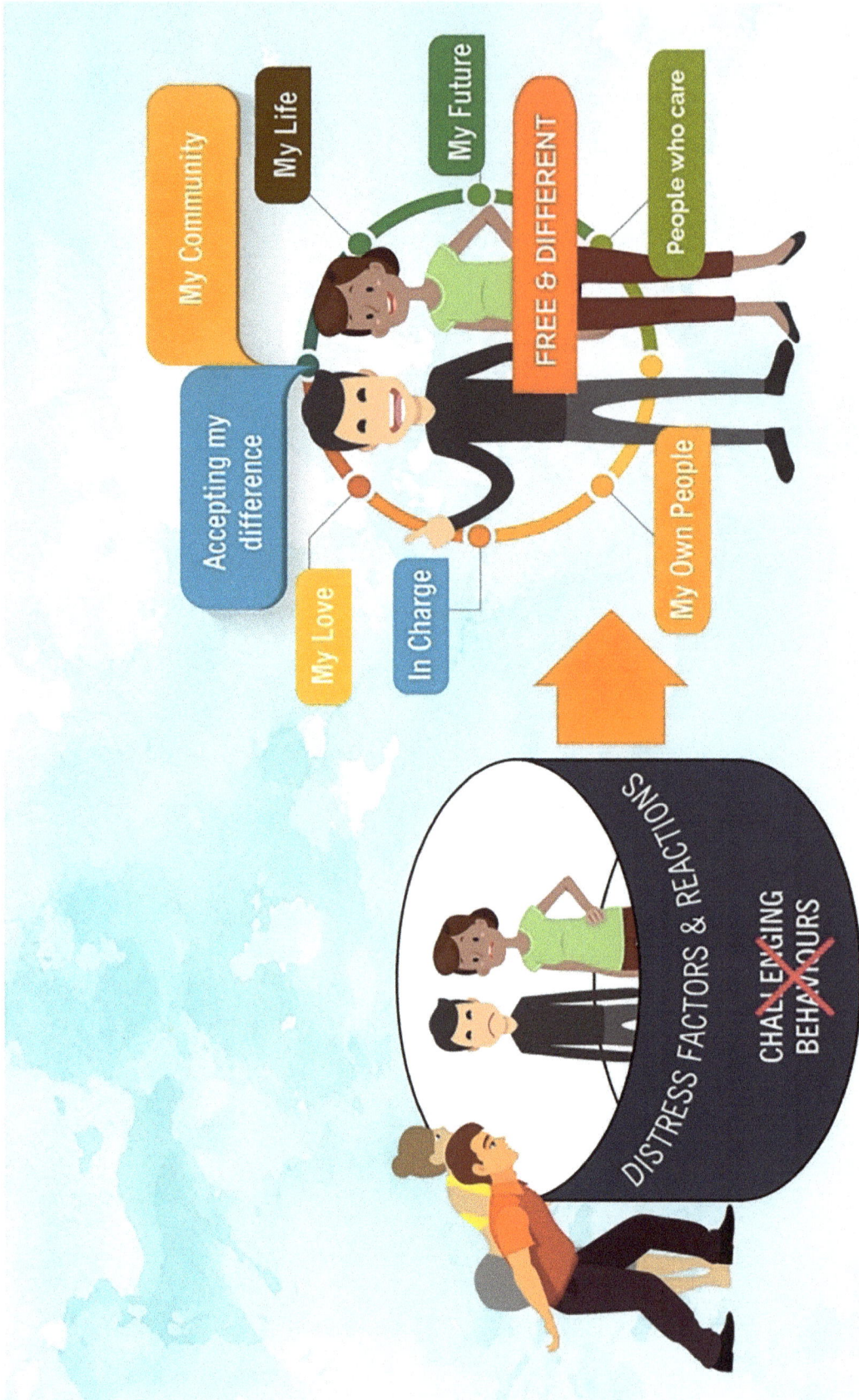

My Community

My Life

My Future

FREE & DIFFERENT

People who care

Accepting my difference

My Love

In Charge

My Own People

DISTRESS FACTORS & REACTIONS

CHALLENGING BEHAVIOURS

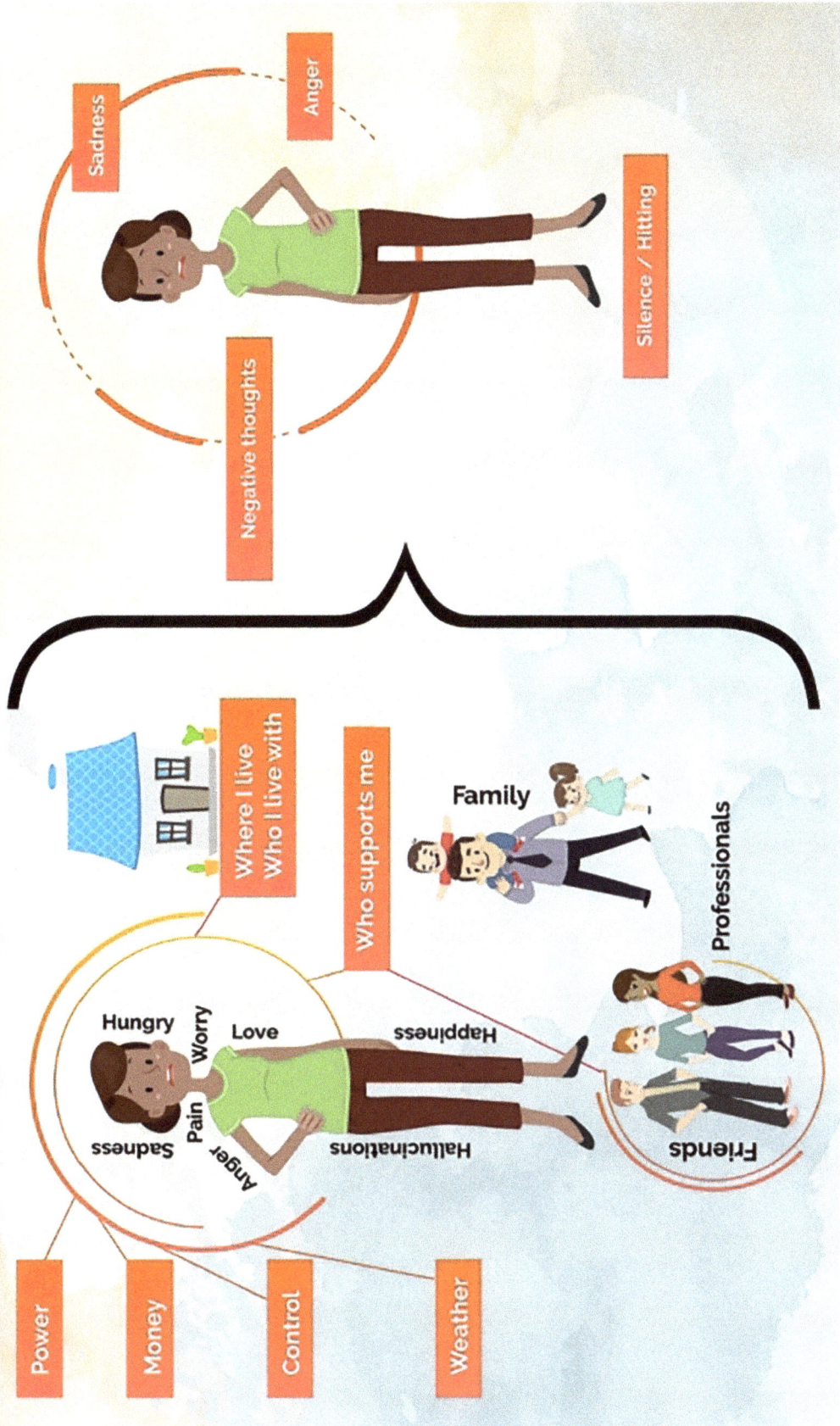

DISTRESS REACTIONS

- Sadness
- Anger
- Silence / Hitting
- Negative thoughts

DISTRESS FACTORS

- Where I live / Who I live with
- Who supports me
- Family
- Professionals
- Friends
- Power
- Money
- Control
- Weather

Hungry · Worry · Love · Pain · Sadness · Anger · Happiness · Hallucinations

On the following page you'll find a letter template to use to explain this step to the person. Please change it as needed. Some people will want to read it, others would prefer a visual adaptation and some will want it read to them. Please use the letter as you want, including writing your name, organisation and address at the top, so that it is clear who it is from. You can also use the pictures.

Remember that it may be too much for someone in distress to have the whole process explained to them. They may be able to cope with an easier-to-understand version or they may not want to know. Please use your judgement.

Dear

I am   and we are worried about you and would like to help you. Please support us to do this. We would like to learn more about you, with your permission. We will be asking some questions and we want to understand your behaviours and thoughts, especially the ones that are not positive for you and can be distressing (difficult, sad) and the reasons for these. Some of the reasons may be *internal* (your history, feelings, and thoughts) and others *external* (where you live).

Once we know, we can work out how to help.

With your permission, we will do this by asking questions. All of this will be done at your pace and time.

Thank you and please let us know if you have any questions.

It's my distress not a challenging behaviour

We have worked with and for adults with challenging behaviours for many years and have done our utmost to help them and their families. Perhaps we did this as we felt empathy with the people for whom we worked.

Looking back on those years, we used the models in which we were trained: functional analysis, cognitive behavioural approaches, etc. The person was analysed, investigated, and recorded through these lenses and the myriad paper documents that these methods created.

There has been an increasing humanisation of the processes so that now we focus more on the whole person; this shift can be seen in the way we have defined this issue. It began as 'behaviours that challenge the system' (TASH) and then 'challenging behaviours' to 'challenges'. However, there is still a tendency to see the person as a range of behaviours which do not fit their current living circumstances, rather than someone who is unhappy or, in extreme circumstances, distressed. What is also interesting is that the term is now applied in other fields, e.g. mental health, older people, and learning difficulties.

The NHS speaks of reducing distress in their approach to working with people with challenging behaviours but their methods, whilst being more holistic, don't place the distress that is experienced at the centre of their approach. Instead, they speak of the need to 'control the behaviour' (NHS Social Care and Support Guide, 2018).

The focus, throughout, has generally been on fixing the person to help them change and live to an externally imposed standard. It is the behaviour that is always defined, recorded, analysed and 'sorted out'. We, as helpers (professionals and carers), often assist the person to try to change and live in a controlled environment that we choose. Yet we are happy to live with our own imperfections and do very little about them. And we often have greater control over our physical environment.

We are suggesting an alternative approach, where the real focus is on the whole person and their life circumstances—where we see the behaviour as truly a response to an internal or external imbalance.

The book is sometimes written from the perspective of a person with distress factors and reactions to remind us of the importance of placing people themselves centre stage.

Terms and terminology

Distress reactions include observable behaviours, e.g. aggression, and those that are unobservable, e.g. hallucinations. They occur as a result of the person's internal factors, e.g. mental health, personal history and/or their interaction with external physical, social and environmental factors. These are the distress factors whose impact will vary.

There can be some circularity between distress factors and reactions, e.g. refusing to participate (reaction) can occur as a result of history (internal factor) and the living environment (external factor). The refusal to participate (reaction) can then spiral into a factor as well, e.g. the person recognises that their behaviour achieves results (people stop asking them to do activities) and therefore feels justified in continuing it.

We are using the phrases 'distress factors' and 'distress reactions' to help us in our thinking. Please do not use these phrases to describe people—their name should suffice.

We also utilise the terms 'learning disabilities' and 'learning difficulties' to describe people with intellectual differences, simply because these terms are commonly used.

What are distress factors and reactions?

The real story	**The service perspective**
How I feel inside makes a difference when I wake up and as I go through the day. I wake up in my home and sometimes I feel very rested and happy and then the radio comes on too loudly or my flatmate shouts and my mood changes. I get out of bed in a grumpy mood, and it takes me longer to wash and have breakfast.	Rhona appears to wake up in a bad mood and it always means that it takes her a long time to get ready and so we have to hurry her up. She is too sensitive to ordinary things. The clinical psychologist has asked us to record the incidence of her behaviours.

Internal and external distress factors

My behaviour and thoughts (distress reactions) depend on my internal and external distress factors, e.g. how I feel inside and how this interacts with the outside world (both factors), and they lead to my reactions—behaviours and thoughts.

These are the factors that lead and currently contribute to internal and external distress reactions. They can include current feelings, personal history (internal) and more practical factors, such as where the person lives (external).

Internal distress factors can include the following thinking:

'I feel ill.'
'I am sad about my life.'
'I have given up on my life.'
'Nobody hears or listens to me.'
'I am remembering bad things that have happened.'
 'I am in pain.'

'I hate being restrained.'

'I am hungry.'

'I am hallucinating.'

'I am very, very anxious.'

'I keep thinking about the same thing.'

'I feel well.'

'I feel happy.'

'I am feeling confident about my life.'

'I remember good things that have happened.'

'I am not hungry.'

'I find it difficult to say and let people know what I want.'

External distress factors include:

Where I live

My partner/family/housemates/flatmates

Who lives with me

Who makes my decisions

Who supports me

Who my neighbours are

Whether I like my doctor, psychologist, managers

How much control I have in my life

The valued things I do, e.g. work

The weather

What is happening in my town, my country, the world

Climate change

How I travel

Traditionally, some of these factors have been described as triggers but these are usually factors located in the immediate present of the person's life rather than longer term issues such as control and history.

Distress reactions happen because internal factors interact with external factors. Distress reactions can include thoughts as well as behaviours.

There can, legitimately, be an overlap between a distress factor and a reaction. Our feelings and behaviours can be circular and feed each other. For example, if a person feels unsafe (internal factor) and is placed in a threatening environment (external factor), they could become aggressive (external distress reaction). They then realise that this behaviour keeps them safe and so they begin to internalise this as a justification (internal factor) for continuing with the distress reaction of aggression, i.e. 'It is safer for me to hit them first. People stay away.' Another example is taking medication (external factor) that leads to negative thoughts (internal reaction and factor).

Internal distress reactions

These can include repetitive thoughts and conclusions such as:

'I hate/like where I live.'
'I really don't have much control over my life and so I give up.'
'I like letting other people manage my life.'
'I feel out of control and so I want to hit out.'
 'I don't like it when they put me in timeout.'
'My voices are telling me to do something awful.'
 'I am not OK with where I am living.'
'I don't like the people I live with.'

External distress reactions

'Sometimes, my behaviour can be very destructive and negative because it is a way of coping with my current life and/or because of something bad that happened to me in my past.'

'Occasionally, I prefer to perpetuate negativity in my life, e.g. "It's easier because I know how to be like this".'

They also include:

hitting
shouting
destroying furniture
manipulating people
speaking and listening to the voices in my head
being very silent and refusing to participate
deliberately harming myself

As you can see, these factors are not unusual but ones that could be experienced. The emphasis is on considering these without the use of technical terms which can dehumanise.

Chapter Two

DECIDING WHETHER OR NOT SOMEONE NEEDS HELP

HELP NEEDED?.

On the following page you'll find a letter template to use to explain this step to the person. Please change it as needed. Some people will want to read it, others would prefer a visual adaptation, and some will want it read to them. Please use the letter as you want. You can also use the picture to explain.

Remember that it may be too much for someone in distress to have the whole process explained to them all at once. They may be able to cope with an easier to understand version or they want the news in stages, or they may not want to know. Please use your judgement.

Hello!

This is the first step in us trying to help you.

We need to ask some questions to make sure that you are safe and then find out what type of help you need now and in the future.

We will go through some questions with you and others who are involved with you. This will give us an idea of how we can help.

Please tell us if we are going too fast and if it is too much. We will stop whenever you want.

Once the questions have been answered, we will tell you what we think, and we would like your advice.

Please tell us if you have any questions.

Thank you.

Professionals often assume that, if a person is behaving unusually, they need to intervene and do something to bring about change. However, it is very important to stop and think about whether help is—or is not—necessary and, if it is, what type of assistance is required. This pause will aid us to ensure that the right supports and solutions are created to aid the person.

Remember that we all have distress reactions that we do nothing about. We also need to think about helping for the long term rather than just for the time of our employment in that service.

Achieving success in changing your life can take time and the definition of accomplishment can vary between the person and the professional.

1998

I, Barbara, live with four of my six children, Steven, Mary, John, and William. I like going out at night and men are nice to me, but I can hit them. The voices tell me what to do and I like it. I don't take the medicine because I forget. The house is full of rubbish, and it is too much, and I can't do anything about it. Mary looks after the others. They are going to take John and William from me like the other two. The house smells and I have no money.

2016

I have managed to keep a clean house for a while now and William, who is 25, lives with me. I live on benefits with a part-time job, and I don't get into trouble with men so much and I take my medicine. Mary does not talk to me; she must be tired of me. John is in a boarding school and comes to stay with me for the holidays. Life is OK.

Comment from professional

Alison, Clinical Psychologist: 'She really could have done more to address her psychological issues earlier and ought to have a full-time job. It's been almost twenty years.'

As noted above, distress reactions include observable behaviours, e.g. aggression, and those that are unobservable, e.g. hallucinations. They occur because of the person's internal condition and/or their interaction with external physical, social and environmental factors. They can include appropriate behaviours and their impact will vary.

First, we must decide if the person needs our help. In the following pages, you will find a range of questions with 'sliding scale' answers, which should assist you. The form templates enable you to build from your initial assessment so that you can consider next steps to take if you believe that an intervention or further help is needed. Remember to involve the person as much as possible.

Deciding whether or not someone needs help

1. What are my distress reactions—behaviours/thoughts?

Please describe them.

Questioner: please use appropriate words to ask the person to rate their distress reactions in terms of severity, intensity, and frequency.

1.

2.

3.

4.

2. What internal and external distress factors may be leading to my distress reactions?

3. Is there a significant risk of harm to me? If yes, do I need to be taken somewhere safe immediately?

4. What impact are my carers and supporters having on my life?

Negative impact -- Positive impact

5. How many people are affected by my distress reactions?

Only me -- Many people

6. How upset am I by my distress reactions?

Happy with the behaviours/thoughts --- Very upset

7. How acceptable are my behaviours/thoughts?

Very much accepted by all --- Not at all accepted

8. What percentage of my time is spent in these behaviours/thoughts?

0% -- 100%

9. How risky are my behaviours/thoughts?

No risk at all --- Very, very risky

10. How many other behaviours/thoughts are present?

None --- Many

11. How aware am I about my behaviours/thoughts?

No awareness --- Very aware

12. How much do I want to change my behaviours/thoughts?

Not at all --- As much as possible

13. How much help do you think I need?

None -- As much help as possible

14.   How much help do I think I need?

None---As much help as possible

15.   Who is motivated to help me? List the people.

16.   Could there be a physical/medical/psychiatric/psychological explanation for my behaviour? If so, what might it be?

17.   How risky are the current interventions that are used to help me?

Not risky--Extremely risky

These questions will help you decide whether or not the person needs/wants to be supported. If the behaviour is not really causing concern or is not very negative, then there may not be any need to intervene.

Now, please write down your conclusions:

NEXT STEPS

If your assessment is that the person needs help, then carefully consider the next steps you can take to support them. If you decide that help is not needed, please double check with someone else that you have reached the best conclusion for the person.

Chapter Three

LEARNING MORE ABOUT THE DISTRESS FACTORS AND REACTIONS

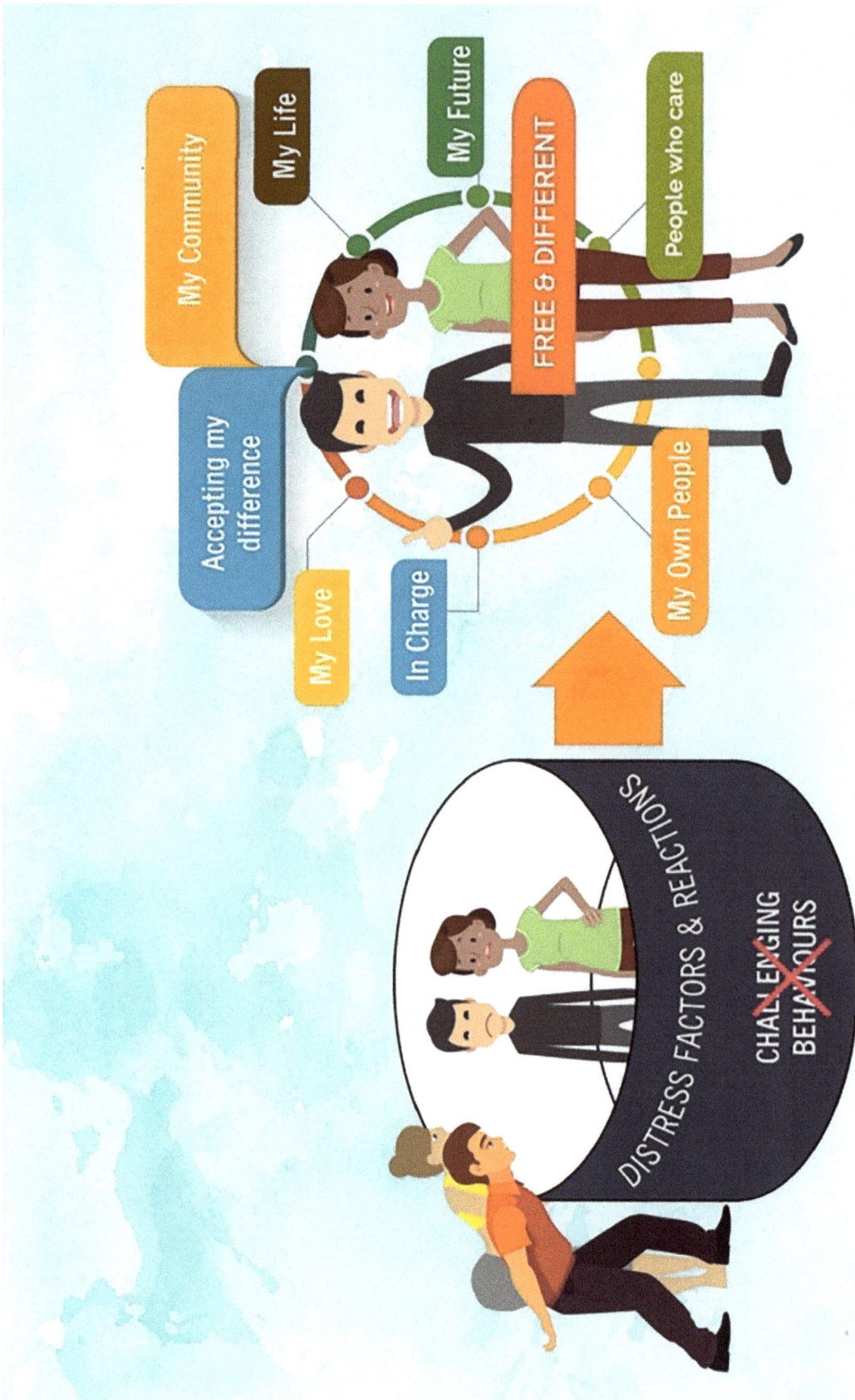

My Community

My Life

My Future

FREE & DIFFERENT

People who care

Accepting my difference

My Love

In Charge

My Own People

DISTRESS FACTORS & REACTIONS

CHALLENGING BEHAVIOURS

Helping Me Understand

FAMILY

JUST WANT TO HELP

FRIENDS

PARTNERS

PAID TO HELP

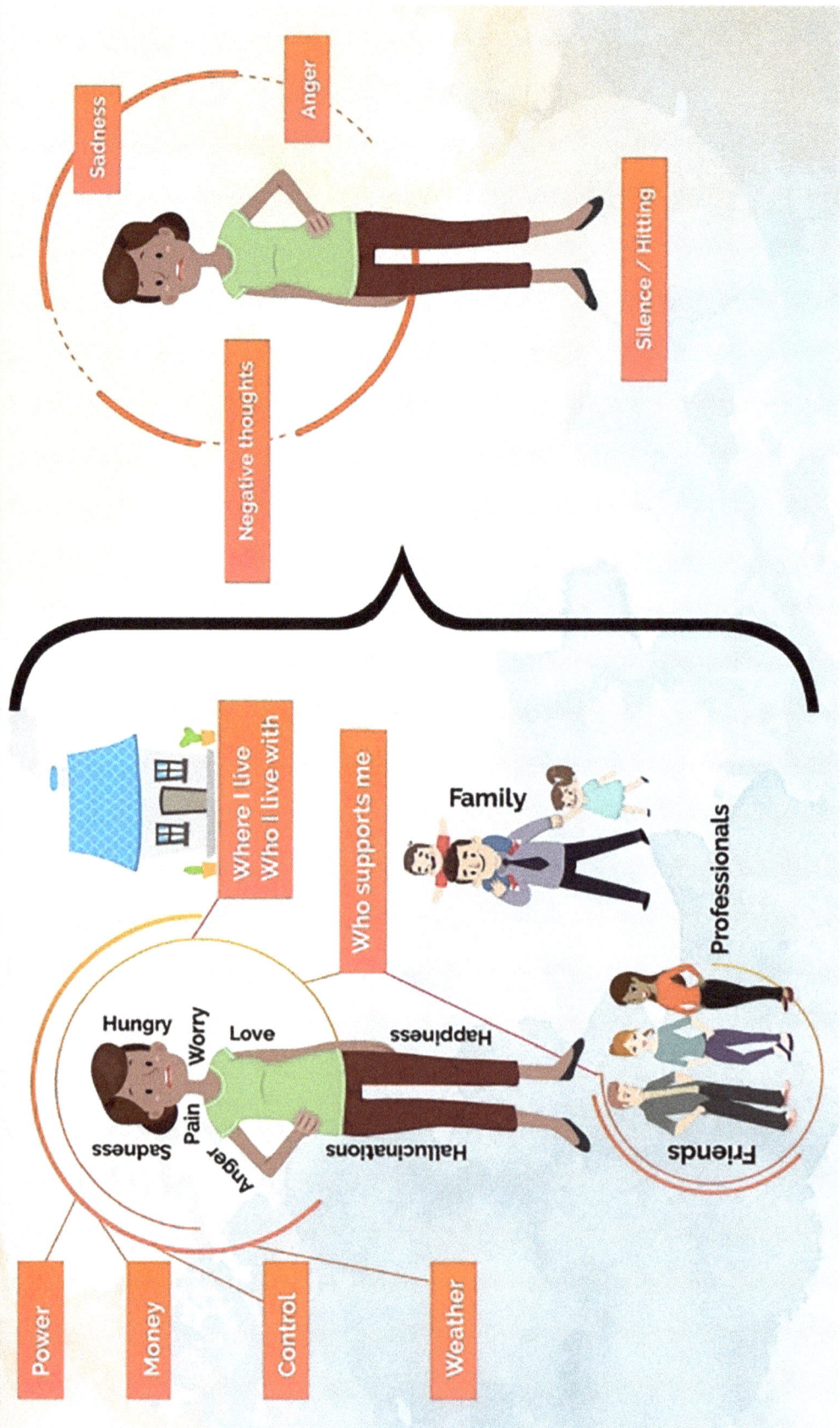

DISTRESS REACTIONS

Sadness
Anger
Silence / Hitting
Negative thoughts

DISTRESS FACTORS

Where I live
Who I live with
Who supports me
Family
Professionals
Friends
Hungry
Worry
Love
Pain
Anger
Sadness
Happiness
Hallucinations
Power
Money
Control
Weather

On the following page is a letter template you can use to explain this step to the person. Please change it as needed. Some people will want to read it, others would prefer a visual adaptation and some will want it read to them. Please use the letter and picture to explain as you want.

Remember that it may be too much for someone in distress to have the whole process explained to them all at once. They may be able to cope with an easier to understand version or they want the news in stages, or they may not want to know. Please use your judgement.

Dear

Now it is important for us to find out more about you and your life and who helps by doing an assessment.

Please give us your permission. We will respect your privacy as much as possible. There are a lot of questions, and we will ask for your help in choosing the right ones.

Once we understand you more fully, we can work with you to develop a plan to help you look at how you are managing and what change is needed.

We will discuss all of our concerns with you. Please tell us if you want to know anything about what we have explained.

Thank you.

Assessment

A good and thorough assessment is absolutely vital. The more information you gather at this stage, the better. It is when we miss the tiny vital clue that we ignore the key to helping the person.

The steps are:

1. Gather as much information as possible about the person using the questions below.

2. Make sure that you have done all that is necessary to keep the person safe while you are investigating.

3. Remember to ask for permission from the person and significant others before starting. If they refuse to participate, explain that the intention is to help and that you will keep them informed. If they persist in refusing, then a decision needs to be made about whether to continue with the assessment. Such decisions need to be taken with the best interests of the person in mind.

4. Make sure that confidentiality is always respected.

5. Start with the person and talk/spend time with them. Follow their lead—they will give you clues if you are prepared to listen, regardless of whether the person communicates verbally or not. Non-verbal behaviour can also tell us so much if we take the time to observe. Pictures can be used to communicate with the person.

6. Talk to those closest to the person to get their answers to the questions below. Remember, there could be different perspectives on the same issue, it is important to record these variations and look for congruence and verification, if possible.

7. Ask some initial questions and then work out if anything needs to be recorded and for how long. Consider that there is often a lot of information about a person, and it may not always be necessary to introduce a great deal of recording.

A listening mindset

We can, especially if we have been trained, come in with a fixed mindset when we are trying to help someone with distress reactions. We need to free our thinking and operate in the most abstract way.

Otto Scharmer outlines four levels at which we can operate:

Level One: Downloading—we ignore what is different in the current situation and simply do what we have done before.

Level Two: Conversational—we notice what is different but ignore this and repeat past actions.

Level Three: Empathising—we pay attention to the difference and change what we did.

Level Four: Emergent—we see what is different and we operate from first principles and listen widely and deeply to what is present and said, and what is unsaid. We create new actions.

We must operate at Level Four and listen out for the clues and hints that others may have ignored.

www.ottoscharmer.com

Focusing on the whole person

It is worth thinking about the type of life that the person wants and the associated standards. It is important to use this as a core thread when looking at what is happening for the person and when creating solutions and plans.

Life standards

What are the life standards that I want (you can use the principles below, or your own, to have this discussion)? What type of citizen do I want to be?

Support and care

We support and care for ourselves and others without being greedy.
We support and look after the planet.
We have positive relationships with friends and family.
We are patient and kind; we do not bully.

Respect

We respect ourselves, each other, and the environment.

Integrity

We live by our values.
We are honest and respectful in everything we say and do.

For future generations

We work towards a more peaceful, conflict-free world where we are all equal. We use our planet's natural resources wisely.

Freedom of heart and mind

We listen to everyone with an open heart and mind.
We are open to other people's views; we try not to judge others.
We feel we can express our emotions.

Hope and courage

We are hopeful and brave.
We take calculated risks.

Productive living and working

We are productive in our communities.

We work and live by these values.

The values I want to live by are:

The kind of citizen I want to be is:

Finding out about the person

Here are a lot of questions that we have devised for you to ask. Remember to select only the important ones. This can be done with the person and those who are central in their life from informal (family, partners, friends) to formal (professionals, GPs, psychologists etc.).

More questions are available in the appendices.

Internal factors

1. What hopes and dreams do I have?

2. What can I do? What do I need help with?

3. How much control in my life do I personally have? What is limiting in my life?

4. How hopeful am I about my life?

5. How ready am I for change?

6. Who likes me?

7. Who respects me?

8. How much is my diversity and cultural background respected?

9. How physically well am I? What medical examinations have been done/ are needed?

10. What medication am I taking? What are the side effects?

11. What diagnosis, if any, do I have? How does it affect my life?

12. What are my allergies?

13. Have I had any accidents that could be affecting me?

14. What special problems might I have, e.g. neurological, psychological, mental health?

    (There are further questions that can be asked in this area—please see Appendices One and Two—these should only be asked by a mental health professional.)

15. What is my personal history? Which events, circumstances could have a positive or negative effect on me now?

16. Have I got a history of living in large institutions and/or in care and/or living with my parents/family for most of my life?

17. How do I communicate? What do you need to learn about how I speak/ listen?

18. How much do I express my emotions appropriately/inappropriately?

19. How do I feel generally?

External factors

1. What food and drink preferences do I have?

2. How affected am I by the climate/weather?

3. How much noise is there in my environment?

4. Where do I live? How much do I like my living situation?

5.   How crowded is my environment?

6.   What is the physical environment like? How does this affect me?

7.   How much access do I have to my money?

8.   Who pays for my living expenses etc.?

9.   What do I do during the day? How fulfilled am I in my daily activities? How meaningful are my activities? What do I actually want to do?

10.   What do I like doing for leisure?

11.   How do I travel around?

12.   What types of clothes do I like?

13.   What do I know about events in my community, town, country, and the world? What impact do these have on my life?

14.   Who has the power and control in my life?

15.   Who are the important people in my life? What types of relationship do I have? What relationships do I want?

16.   Who supports me informally? Who is paid to support me? How beneficial are these relationships? How good is the quality of my support? How well do my supporters know and understand me? (Other organisational questions are available in Appendix Three.)

17.   Who hates me? Who likes me?

The distress reactions

Here are some questions to help you learn about the reactions.

1. What is the behaviour/thought that is of concern? (Remember there can be more than one.)

2. Who is concerned? Why?

3. What explanation do I give for my behaviour/thought?

4. What is known about why I carry out the behaviour?

5. What are the internal factors that contribute?

6. What are the external factors that contribute?

7. What are the interactions between internal and external factors?

8. What are the risks that are involved? How are these currently addressed? Are these interventions adequate?

9. What level of upset is experienced by me and significant others when I demonstrate this behaviour?

10. How acceptable is the behaviour in my community and wider society? What adjustments have had to be made to accommodate my behaviour?

11. How much of my time is spent in this behaviour and thoughts?

12. What solutions have been tried (including physical restraint)? What has worked and could continue? What should be stopped?

13. What are the crisis plans? What should be the crisis plans?

14. What solutions are/would be acceptable to me?

15. What fears and concerns do I have about change?

16. What will help me with altering my behaviour if change is needed?

17. What is the ability of significant others and supporters to cope? What help will they need?

18. What organisational issues affect me? What needs to change? (There are more organisational questions in Appendix Three.)

19. What environmental changes need to be made?

20. What is positive about my life?

21. What are the priority actions for change?

22. What needs to stay the same?

23. What needs to be recorded?

Recording

Recording is often seen as essential, but these systems reflect the current emphasis on behaviours and can limit the perceptions of the distress reactions. For example, ABC charts ask you to record what happens just before, during and after the behaviour has occurred. These records may miss the fact that a person is in pain and cannot articulate that fact except by being aggressive whenever they are asked to move.

It is far better to simply spend time with the person and their supporters so you can get to know them. Visually record the person, with their permission. Once you have spent time and/or have a visual record of the person, reflect on what you have learned especially in terms of being able to answer the questions above. Sometimes, a simple diary will be helpful; but this must be completed with the permission of the person or their advocate.

Learning more about the person

Once you have spent a significant amount of time learning about and understanding the person, complete this form.

What life standards does the person have?

What are the key *internal* factors?

What are the key *external* factors?

What are the interactions between distress factors and reactions?

What have we learned about the person's distress reactions?

WORKING OUT WHAT IS HAPPENING

Helping Me Understand

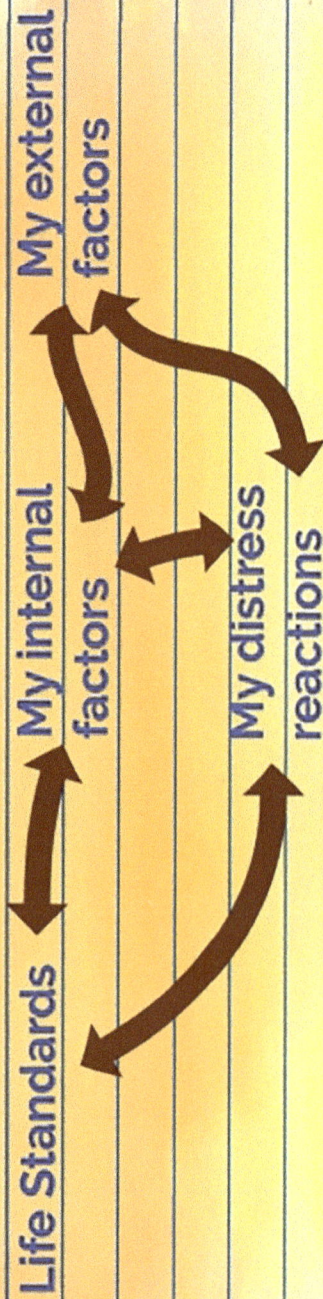

Life Standards

My internal factors

My external factors

My distress reactions

Most important things we have learned

• • • • •

On the following page you'll find a letter template to use to explain this step to the person. Please change it as needed. Some people will want to read it, others would prefer a visual adaptation and some will want it read to them. Please use the letter and picture, as you want, to explain.

Remember that it may be too much for someone in distress to have the whole process explained to them all at once. They may be able to cope with an easier to understand version or they want the news in stages, or they may not want to know. Please use your judgement.

Dear

Now it is time to work out what are the most important concerns for you and your life. We think these are:

1.

2.

3.

4.

5.

Please let us know what you think of these and what changes you would like. Thank you.

Go through all of the information with key people (including the person themselves). (If it is not possible to have the person present, then please have a picture of the person in a prominent place in the room and on the wall chart.) Depict all the information on a huge wall chart. Show the video records if you have them.

Ask the group to reflect on the wall chart and highlight what they **notice**. Once they have done that, ask the group to take a break to think about what they have **not noticed**.

Then work with the group to answer the following questions in relation to the person:

What are my hopes and dreams?

What are my life standards?

What lifestyle would make me happy?

What will help me feel safe during any change?

What are the positive aspects of my current life?

Who/what is helping me?

Who/what is hindering me?

How much motivation is there for change—me and key individuals?

What is the pattern of the distress reaction? What are the clues? What triggers the reaction?

Why is this distress reaction being demonstrated? What are the key internal and external factors? What medical/psychological/psychiatric reason could there be? What other behaviours/facts need to be considered?

What has been tried before?

What is needed for a good solution to help me?

What are the risks?

What organisational issues need to be tackled?

What resources are available?

What life do I want and deserve?

There are a lot of questions, so please select the most important. And remember it is always worth repeating an issue to make sure you really understand the person.

Having had the discussions, first outline the priority concerns for the person—please list from Most important [1] to Least important [5]. We often have a huge list of issues that require interventions. It is so important to only highlight the vital issues. Think about the fact that most of us don't want to adjust and that change is usually best if it is incremental. Please remember that basic needs must be met first, such as a decent place to live.

My priority list of concerns

1.

2.

3.

4.

5.

Remember to work at Listening Level Four: Emerging, i.e. seeing this as a brand-new situation. Ask the person to comment/react to your conclusions.

Chapter Five

CREATING A PLAN FOR AND WITH THE PERSON

Helping Me

Life Standards
Helping me

My hopes and dreams

The life I deserve

Distress Reactions
Why
Pattern
Solutions (Past)

Life style for happiness
Positive aspects

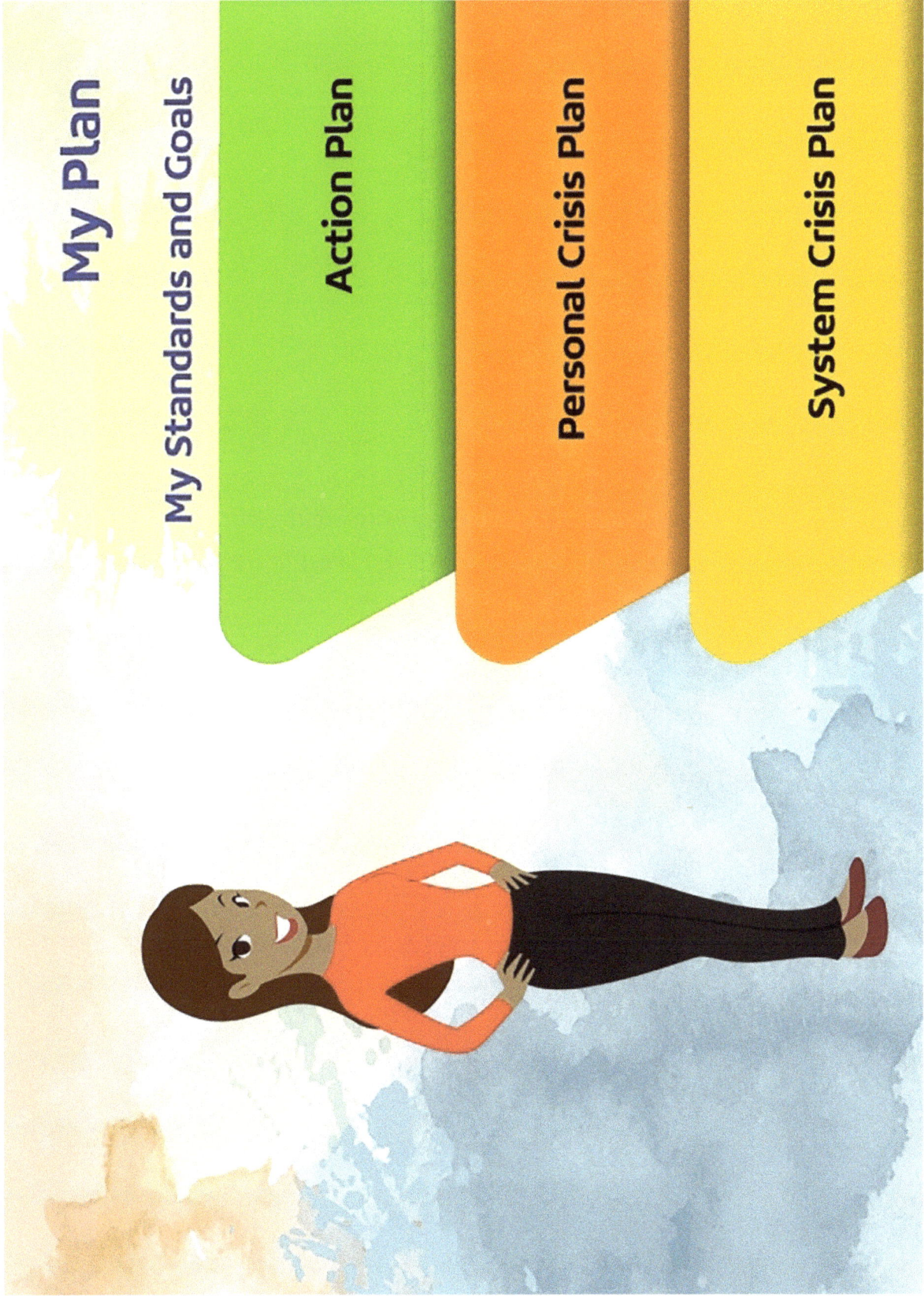

My Plan

My Standards and Goals

Action Plan

Personal Crisis Plan

System Crisis Plan

On the following page you'll find a letter template to use to explain this step to the person. Please change it as needed. Some people will want to read it, others would prefer a visual adaptation, and some will want it read to them. Please use the letter and pictures as you want, including writing your name, organisation and address at the top, so that it is clear who the letter is from.

Remember that it may be too much for someone in distress to have the whole process explained to them all at once. They may be able to cope with an easier to understand version or they want the news in stages, or they may not want to know. Please use your judgement.

Note: *The letter refers to a table. This is included at the end of this chapter.*

Dear

Let's work together to create a plan to help you. We would like to meet with
to do the planning. Would you like to attend?
What will help you attend and stay in the meeting? What support will you need if
you want to leave the meeting?

If you do not want to be present, then tell us please. We will make sure that your
views are heard, and we will tell you what was talked about.

Here is a table of what we will be discussing.

Thank you once again and we look forward to working with you.

This plan should focus on helping the person gain a different lifestyle that is more in line with their hopes and dreams, and which ensures that they are treated with respect and dignity and as full members of our society. It should be based on all of the information that you have already gathered. Ideally, this should be done at a meeting of all concerned including, if possible, the person themselves. Some parts may be done at smaller meetings depending on individual comfort levels.

There are three parts of the plan:

1. Understanding what **standards and goals** the person wants

2. Building an **action plan** to help with the distress reactions

3. Creating **a plan for crisis situations**

1. Standards and goals

Having identified the key concerns for the person, ask them what they would like as goals for their life. The key consideration is to support the person to live a full life. Involve the person and their supporters in identifying the key outcomes/positive goals that will help them to live the fullest possible life.

Key values to consider are:

Support and care
Respect
Integrity
Concern for future generations
Freedom of heart and mind
Hope and courage
Productive living and working

Ask:

What are this person's life standards and goals? Remember the answers as you are completing the plans.

2. Action plan

Here are the steps to creating the plan for the person and their future life.

Obtain an overview of the vital information to inform the plan, including key concerns.
Prioritise the key actions and think about the possible overlaps.
Create crisis plans for the person, their supporters, and the organisation around them.

Standards, goals and action plan for distress factors and reactions

Please return to the earlier discussions and summarise them. Then complete this table at a meeting of concerned and relevant people including the person themselves. If they cannot be present, then please have a photograph of them in a prominent place and ensure that they have been consulted.

Area	Expected outcome for me	Action and person/organisation responsible
Reactions: what I want to change (behaviours/thoughts)		
My life standards and goals		
Internal factors (ways of addressing them)		
External factors (ways of addressing them)		
Interactions between internal and external factors		

Action chart

Discuss what impact the actions will have on each other and whether they will really lead to the person fulfilling their version of citizenship. You can also use a GANTT chart to look at the timeframe within which actions need to take place and the order in which they should occur. Here is a sample GANTT chart.

Action	Month 1	Month 2	Month 3	Month 4	Month 5
A	Start date			End date	
B		Start date			End date
C					
D					
E					

Learning to listen

There is no readily available list of solutions and interventions that we can offer. Experience tells us that the more the needs of the person are at the centre of our thinking, the more likely it is that we will find a good resolution.

> **Kieran** *really liked to investigate any electrical socket, light, or device that he came across. His professional staff felt creative and decided to employ an electrician to work with him as one of his support staff. Only after doing this, did they ask Kieran what he wanted to do with his time—he said that he wanted to be a gardener…*

We have learned that it is important to acknowledge that, while it is extremely unlikely that we can give the person exactly the life they need both practically and psychologically, we can help to provide the best alternative.

> **Saj** *hated closed doors and cupboards, partly because of his history. Staff working with him found an apartment that he liked and they made changes to it so that it became open plan without doors.*

It is vital to acknowledge that distress reactions, especially for adults, will not disappear overnight especially if a change is imposed, as it often is. The distress reactions are often an indication of the person's strength of character; they may well also be protecting themselves and, therefore, they are likely to maintain their old behaviour initially. Additionally, change is difficult for many of us and we do not generally easily accept it if it is imposed upon us.

> **Petra** *liked arguing a lot and staff decided that, instead of arguing back, they would carry a card that said, 'We can talk later'. Times were allocated in the day for these discussions. Initially, Petra continued to argue until staff helped her think about what else she could discuss that was of interest to her. Petra also learned the difference between being argumentative and assertive.*

This is why it is important to understand the person's expectations and motivations for change. The action plan should take these factors into account.

If, for some reason, the plan is not effective after a while, then it is better to acknowledge this and try to understand why it is not working and produce a more reasonable set of actions.

> **Aysha***, a woman with Autism, liked to 'escape' from her locked facility to steal food. The interventions that had been in place focused on ways of keeping her in and restricting access to food. A plan was created to enable Aysha to leave the facility daily and go for walks but her interest in food was not addressed. Consequently, the walks became a daily fight. The decision was taken to help Aysha by first ensuring that there was no medical reason for her interest in food and then facilitating greater access to food while at the same time making plans to help her move to a more ordinary place to live.*

Please remember that our definition of success may not match that of the person. Stop and think about what the person actually wants and try to achieve that. For example, having a bedroom that is green and red with orange and blue furniture may be exactly what the person wants and desires. It may not be to our taste, but we should facilitate what people want for themselves, as we are all individual.

As fellow human beings, we know that change takes time and can be slow. It is the same patience we need to have when we are helping someone with distress factors and reactions implement a plan to alter their approaches and life.

3. Crisis plans: personal and system

A very clear crisis plan for the person should be written with those who would implement it. Please answer these questions to help you build the plan.

What is the behaviour of concern?

What risks are associated with the behaviour? What is the worst that could happen?

Where and when could it happen? What could be the warning signs?

What is needed to address the risks at each stage (before, during and afterwards)?

What resources are needed to address each potential crisis?

What are the safest actions to take?

Physical restraints and timeouts

Physical restraints and timeouts are used a lot in services for people with challenging behaviours, especially if a person's distress reactions include physical aggression or self-harm. They are not ideal solutions because using them usually means that the carers and supporters have lost control of the situation and want it back. Additionally, being restrained is commonly, for the person, an extremely frightening experience. Furthermore, sometimes, these interventions have the opposite effect to that which is desired, e.g. one of our clients came to like going to the timeout room because he got a lot of physical contact on the way there and then peace and quiet for a while when in the room.

It is true that, sometimes, someone has to be held (appropriately) for their own good, e.g. helping them to calm down. However, it is vital that the whole pattern and build up to the distress reaction is investigated thoroughly and steps taken to prevent escalation alongside having techniques available if all else fails.

Remember to create this crisis plan with the person by completing the following form, 'Personal crisis plan'.

As well a personal crisis plan, one for the system (organisation, managers, carers and supporters) is also usually required. Create this 'System crisis plan' with those who will be supporting the person.

You can find photocopiable templates of both plans on the following pages.

Personal crisis plan

Stage	How I could behave	How to help me
Pre-crisis (including warning signs)		
Crisis		
Post-crisis		

System crisis plan

Stage	Associated risks and benefits for organisation, managers, carers and supporters	Actions to be taken
Pre-crisis (including warning signs)		
Crisis		
Post-crisis		

Planning for crises—the before and the after

Crises are composed of stages, and it is vital to plan for each one. There are, usually, many warning signs in the pre-crisis stage that are ignored, e.g. person not taking their medication regularly, staff inconsistency and so on. Plans need to be made not only for the crisis but also for the post-crisis aftermath when all involved will need support.

Remember that the more experienced you are, the more you are likely to underestimate the level of risk involved. If you are stressed, conversely, you are less likely to take a risk.

All those implementing the plans should agree to them. Everyone should feel comfortable with all of the steps to be taken. Rehearse the actions in the plan before it is finalised.

And finally, here is a summary table to be completed. You can use this as part of the letter for the person.

3. Summary of outcomes and actions

Area	Expected outcome for me	Action and person/ organisation responsible
Reactions: what I want to change (behaviours/thoughts)		
My life standards and goals		
Internal factors (ways of addressing them)		
External factors (ways of addressing them)		
Interactions between internal and external factors		
Personal crisis plan (How I am likely to behave, how to help me pre-crisis (warning signs), crisis, postcrisis)		
System crisis plan (Identify risks and benefits for precrisis, crisis and post-crisis, select actions to support the person)		

Progress review date: ....

CASE STUDIES

Here are two fictitious case studies that we have developed. We use them to show you how to use the forms that we created. What follows is our interpretation of the case studies. What would be yours?

Case study one

Background information

Suzanna is 25 years old. She is the middle child in a family of a single parent. Her father left with her youngest sibling, Fred, who was five. Here is her story.

My mother always told me, in many ways, that I was useless. In fact, she preferred my eldest sister, June, to me. I was in a special class at school learning cooking and such while June came first or second, in the ordinary class, all the time.

Mum did not have much money sometimes and so she would ask us to steal from family, friends, and shops. We only got caught twice and the police let us go. They felt sorry for us.

One of Mum's boyfriends moved in when I was ten and he would find ways of isolating me and do, as he said, 'the needful' (sex). He said I had to pay for the money he gave Mum. This stopped when I was thirteen because I accidentally hit him, and he tripped and fell. He was ill afterwards, and I found that threatening people is a good way to live. I didn't tell anyone what he did because he threatened me.

I left Mum's when I was eighteen and moved into a flat with my sister who is working, and she is always out. I don't have a job and no money except for my benefits. I have few friends; people stay away except for Bobba at the pub below us. I have been going to the pub for the last seven years. Bobba and I met last year, and he likes me and will sometimes buy me drinks but now I must kiss him in the toilets for that. Bobba also now likes it when I get aggressive. He is my best friend and sometimes carries me home after the pub when I find it difficult to walk which is most nights. Sometimes we have parties in the flat which my sister does not like. We have been doing this for the last year.

My sister has told Social Services and my social worker has said that I need to stop and be more responsible. Nonsense. The pub has banned me, and the police have been called to the flat many times.

The following is an example of how one might complete the form in this case.

Deciding whether or not someone needs help

1.   What are my distress reactions—behaviours/thoughts?

Please describe them. Please rate them in terms of severity, intensity, and frequency.

1.   *Problems with alcohol*
2.   *Aggressive behaviour*

2.   What internal and external distress factors may be leading to my distress reactions?

Internal—low self-esteem and self-respect
External—living conditions, proximity to the pub, not having a meaningful daily occupation
Limited social life and support

3.   Is there a significant risk of harm to me? If yes, do I need to be taken somewhere safe immediately?

There is a high degree of risk given the tendency to be aggressive necessitating removal to a place of safety as requested by the sister. Emergency accommodation has been found.

4. What impact are my carers and supporters having on my life?

Negative impact --------------------------- X --------------------------- Positive impact

Sister—does care but is tired of trying to help. She wants to get on with her own life. Bobba has a very negative impact, but Suzanna does not acknowledge this.

5. How many people are affected by my distress reactions?

Only me --- X ---------------Many people

Many are affected. She has a negative reputation in the area as the one who fights.

6. How upset am I by my distress reactions?

Happy with the behaviours/thoughts -------------------- X --------------- Very upset

Now that the difficulties have been pointed out, she is becoming upset at the realisation of the impact of her behaviour.

7. How acceptable are my behaviours/thoughts?

Very much accepted by all --------------------------------X-------- Not at all accepted

Neither her behaviour nor her thoughts are acceptable.

8. What percentage of my time is spent in these behaviours/thoughts?

0% --------------------------------X--- 100%

Approximately 40% of her time is spent in these behaviours.

9.   How risky are my behaviours/thoughts?

No risk at all ----------------------------------- X ---------------------Very, very risky

Some risk to her health and the aggression can be very risky, hence the removal to a safer location.

10.   How many other behaviours/thoughts are present?

None ---- X --- Many

No other problems have been reported.

11.   How aware am I about my behaviours/thoughts?

No awareness --------------------------- X -------------------------------------Very aware

Suzanna has a growing awareness of her problems.

12.   How much do I want to change my behaviours/thoughts?

Not at all ------------------------ X ---------------------------------As much as possible

Suzanna's willingness to change is limited as the need to recognise the problems has been instigated by others not herself.

13.   How much help do you think I need?

None --- X -------------As much help as possible

She needs professional help.

14. How much help do I think I need?

None----------------- X ------------------------------------- As much help as possible

She thinks that seeing a counsellor and finding a new flat will be enough.

15. Who is motivated to help me? List them.

Only her sister and her support is limited.

Bobba may help but his motives are questionable.

16. Could there be a physical/medical/psychiatric/psychological explanation for my behaviour? If so, what might it be?

There is a history of abuse and a possible addiction to alcohol. She has limited life skills.

17. How risky are the current interventions that are used to help me?

Not risky -------------------------------------- X ---------------------- Extremely risky

There are no key formal interventions in place, only the fact that Suzanna's sister called Social Services.

Now, please write down your conclusions:

Suzanna needs to have a formal psychological, psychiatric, and medical evaluation to understand her background and then determine the extent of her liking/addiction to alcohol as well as an assessment of her life and social skills. A determination also needs to be made about her living conditions and support needs.

NEXT STEPS

If your assessment is that the person needs help, then carefully consider the next steps you can take to support them. If you decide that help is not needed, please double check with someone else that you have reached the best conclusion for the person.

Learning more about the person

What life standards does the person have?

She has limited life standards beyond, perhaps, a desire for immediate gratification.

Her self-esteem is low, and she does not think that she can succeed at anything as she keeps comparing herself to her sister.

What are the key internal factors?

Recurrent feelings of low self-worth

History of abuse

Feeling that she will never be like her sister who is now a professional manager.

Wariness of letting people get close to her because of the abuse in her background and the approach taken by her mother.

What are the key external factors?

Living with her sister reminds her daily that she is not 'worth that much'.

Limited social support, except from Bobba whose care is negative.

Inadequate meaningful daily occupation.

What are the interactions between distress factors and reactions?

Her fighting and refusal to stop drinking and seeing Bobba reinforce her low self-worth which was probably built by her past abuse and upbringing.

What have we learned about the person's distress reactions?

Her aggression is a learned response which has a large protective factor and keeps people away from her.

Her addiction to alcohol may be driven in part by the need to be occupied and liked by someone. She probably has not realised how detrimental the behaviour is to herself (emotionally and physically) and to the relationship with her sister.

Priority list of concerns

1. *Her addiction*

2. *Her psychological issues and the impact these have on her daily life*

3. *Limited skills for life*

4. *Limited social support*

The intervention plan

Area	Expected outcome for me	Action and person/ organisation responsible
Reactions: what I want to change (behaviours/thoughts)	To respect myself better Not drink Stop hitting people	Suzanna to work with others to build plans described below.
My life standards and goals	I want to respect myself more. I want to look after myself better and have good friends.	Suzanna, with support from her support worker who will help her carry out her self-help action plan including learning about making and keeping good friends.
Internal factors (ways of addressing them)	Increased feelings of self-worth Addressing addiction to alcohol	Suzanna to be admitted into a residential substance misuse facility and to leave with a good relapse prevention and recovery plan. Suzanna to have ongoing counselling while she is an inpatient and to be continued in the community. To learn life coping skills.

External factors (ways of addressing them)	Find a more suitable place to live	Social worker to support her to find a new place to live and arrange for support.
	Seek a more meaningful occupation	Suzanna to work with support staff to further develop her life learning skills by creating a self-help care plan that she follows.
		Suzanna to explore different occupational options.
Interactions between internal and external factors	Learn about how low self-worth may interact with how Suzanna chooses to live and where she wants to live.	Suzanna to have regular discussions with her therapist so she can reflect on the extent to which she is improving her self-respect.
Personal crisis plan (How I am likely to behave, how to help me pre-crisis (warning signs), crisis, post-crisis)	To encourage her to remain in treatment, limit contact with Bobba and follow relapse prevention and recovery plan.	Suzanna to be given emergency contact numbers to call if she feels like relapsing. Reminders of her plan to be discreetly placed in her phone and home.
System crisis plan (Identify risks and benefits for pre-crisis, crisis and post-crisis, select actions to support the person)	Help her to remain in treatment and be supported by relevant professionals on a regular and emergency basis.	Professionals to establish a coordination pathway for her for the duration, i.e. as long as is needed.

Progress review date: Weekly meeting for the first three months and then biweekly.

Case study two

Background information

Jolyon is 45 years old. He moved into a group home five years ago. He is a man with Asperger's who has two focused interests: watching trains and making jam. He was living with his parents and moved when they became unable to support him. He speaks using an electronic communication board.

He sees his family once a month, and via Skype, as they live 200 miles away. The professionals decided that he needed a specialist facility for people with Autism and one was not available nearby.

He likes to have a daily routine and becomes very upset if there is a sudden deviation. His social worker had provided the house manager with a thorough list of all of Jolyon's special requirements and needs.

All was well with his life until there was a change of management at the home six months ago. The new manager, Dan, said that he does not believe in communication boards and that it is too expensive for Jolyon to have with him all the time. Jolyon is now only allowed access to the board twice a day. Dan has also said Jolyon should be expected to follow the overall routine of the house and not his own. Following a very lengthy outing to the local train station, Dan has stipulated that there should be no more visits to stations unless it is for travel. Staff have been told not to speak about these changes to anyone outside the home.

Jolyon has become very withdrawn and is refusing to leave his room. All his meals are brought to him. Jolyon now tends to become aggressive if someone tries to get him to leave his room except for going to the bathroom. He has stopped interacting with people who live in the home, as well as staff.

The manager ensures that Jolyon has access to his communication board when there are visitors. There is always a staff member present because of 'concerns' about his possible aggression. His family have not been able to visit as much.

The local Health and Social Care team have been asked to be involved. A case conference is held, and the house manager says that he is mystified about why Jolyon's behaviour has become worse. He says that they are following all of the agreed plans. He reluctantly agrees to have an assistant psychologist visit to do some observations and to share the ABC charts that have been kept. The Assistant Psychologist (Andy) does some observation and analyses the charts. Andy has noticed that the charts tend to be filled in by the same one or two people. Andy informs his supervisor and then conducts the assessment.

Deciding whether or not someone needs help

1.   What are my distress reactions—behaviours/thoughts?

Please describe them. Please rate them in terms of severity, intensity, and frequency.

1.   *Isolating self*

2.   *Refusal to participate*

3.   *Being inflexible*

4.   *Aggression when asked to do something*

2.   What internal and external distress factors may be leading to my distress reactions?

Jolyon may be missing his family and the old manager.

3.   Is there a significant risk of harm to me? If yes, do I need to be taken somewhere safe immediately?

There is no significant risk of harm as Jolyon spends a large amount of time isolating himself.

4.   What impact are my carers and supporters having on my life?

Negative impact ---X ----------- Positive impact

They are all trying to help as much as possible.

5.   How many people are affected by my distress reactions?

Only me -----------X --Many people

He isolates himself and so not many are affected.

6.   How upset am I by my distress reactions?

Happy with the behaviours/thoughts ---------X----------------------------- Very upset

Jolyon likes to be alone.

7.   How acceptable are my behaviours/thoughts?

Very much accepted by all ---------------------X ------------------- Not at all accepted

Isolation is an unusual tactic but generally acceptable.

8.   What percentage of my time is spent in these behaviours/thoughts?
0% ---X----------------------------- 100%

9. How risky are my behaviours/thoughts?

No risk at all -----------X --Very, very risky

10. How many other behaviours/thoughts are present?

None --------------------X --- Many

11. How aware am I about my behaviours/thoughts?

No awareness-----------X ---Very aware

12. How much do I want to change my behaviours/thoughts?

Not at all----------------------X------------------------------------As much as possible

He likes spending time in his room.

13. How much help do you think I need?

None--X -------------------As much help as possible

14. How much help do I think I need?

None ----------X ---As much help as possible

15. Who is motivated to help me? List them.

The Health and Social Care team

The home manager and staff

16. Could there be a physical/medical/psychiatric/psychological explanation for my behaviour? If so, what might it be?

He does not adjust well to change.

17. How risky are the current interventions that are used to help me?

Not risky ----------X --- Extremely risky

The staff are trying to help as much as possible.

Now, please write down your conclusions:

Jolyon would benefit from a further analysis and a different plan to help him adjust to change. This is then agreed at the team meeting and the assistant psychologist is asked to proceed to the next stage with the home manager.

NEXT STEPS

If your assessment is that the person needs help, then carefully consider the next steps you can take to support them. If you decide that help is not needed, please double check with someone else that you have reached the best conclusion for the person.

Learning more about the person

What life standards does the person have?
He likes to be by himself.

What are the key internal factors?
Jolyon prefers his own company.

What are the key external factors?
Staff changes and less contact with his family have led to this situation.

What are the interactions between distress factors and reactions?
None.

What have we learned about the person's distress reactions?
Jolyon does not adjust well to change and now tends to isolate himself and he can become aggressive even when asked to carry out simple activities.

Priority list of concerns

1. *His inflexibility*

2. *His tendency to be aggressive.*

As we can see, the Health and Social Care team are working with the information that is available to them. This is what sometimes happens and, even if there are suspicions and concerns, there is little that can be done unless someone speaks out about what is actually going on. In the absence of new knowledge, the intervention plan would have focused on trying to make Jolyon more flexible and sociable. There would have been little focus on working with the staff. Overall, it is doubtful that this plan would have succeeded.

Let's assume that one of the staff informs the Assistant Psychologist of exactly what is going on. The staff member also shares a copy of the new instructions that the new home manager, Dan, has issued.

These actions will lead to a very different plan. These need to be discussed with the provider who oversees the home to determine the next steps. Here are some options:

1.   Dan is removed from the management of the home and the old system of support for Jolyon is revised and reinstated.

2.   Dan is admonished, asked to have further education about people with Asperger's and be more closely supervised. The old ways of supporting Jolyon are updated and used.

3.   Jolyon moves to another place with his knowledge and permission.

Throughout this, Jolyon should be given time to recover and rest and have opportunities to rebuild trust in the staff who are paid to be support him. He and his family should also be given an apology for the way in which he was treated. *(This has never happened in our experience but is something that should occur.)*

At this point, another briefer, assessment should be conducted. Here is a draft outline of the plan that would then be constructed assuming that Jolyon remains in the house and Dan stays.

Area	Expected outcome for me	Action and person/organisation responsible
Reactions: what I want to change (behaviours/thoughts)	People to let me do my things my way. People to understand me.	Jolyon to work with Assistant Psychologist and house manager to devise training and update his plans.
My life standards and goals	My supporters are nice to me and respect me.	Provider and house manager have training and supervision on supporting people with Asperger's. A clear support plan is devised and used.
Internal factors (ways of addressing them)	I regain my freedom and self-respect.	Jolyon to have continuous access to his communication board. Jolyon is shown how to deal with any problems that may occur. Jolyon to be involved in the development of his new support plan.
External factors (ways of addressing them)	Supporters to know and understand my differences. Always have clear access to my communication device. Have a way of letting someone know if things change for the worse.	Staff and manager to be trained in how to work with Jolyon. Access to his communication device always is provided and recorded.

Interactions between internal and external factors		
Personal crisis plan (How I am likely to behave, how to help me pre-crisis (warning signs), crisis, post-crisis)	Warning signs are known and acted on.	Staff receive training on Jolyon's warning signs and actions to take at all stages of a crisis.
System crisis plan (Identify risks and benefits for pre-crisis, crisis and post-crisis, select actions to support the person)	Staff understand his warning signs and triggers. Support plans are followed.	Staff given clear training on Jolyon's possible behaviours and ways of helping him. Regular rigorous checks are done to ensure his support plan is being properly implemented.

Progress review date: Weekly meetings and then monthly, as needed.

Chapter seven

STORIES

These are fictional stories of what could happen to someone with distress reactions depending on the support they may get. They are all written in the first person so that we can have a closer sense of what it might be like to be someone in these situations.

Marie

"I was the youngest of my family and the only girl. My parents had waited a long time for me, and I know I was a disappointment. I can't speak a lot and I hurt myself so much. I like to dig holes in my arms and other places. I don't know why but I keep doing this especially when I feel bad and sad or think. Digging helps me to stop thinking and then picking the scabs also makes me feel better.

I used to live with my family, and I liked that except for the nights when my cousin Jenny used to visit. She used to ask to sleep in my bed because she wanted to help me. My parents said yes because they thought I was lonely and wanted to have a sleepover friend. When I was ten, Jenny would stroke my hands, feet, and then other places. She would make me do things. She told me I was dirty and that nobody would believe me if I told. I tried to show my Mum, but she laughed and said I was lying.

I became too much for my parents and I was moved to a specialist unit for people with self-injury. They had a ward round for me when I came. I was allowed to join at the last five minutes when they told me what they would do. They had read all my notes: long history of self-injury, intense dislike of being touched, not able to make relationships especially with women. They said that I had a long history of these behaviours and that they would help me stop.

They started a chart to record when I would hurt myself. They tried to teach me social skills to help me make friends with women. None of this worked and the staff changed a lot. Now they have sedated me, and I must wear gloves all the time that I cannot remove. That is all that has changed.

Why don't they find a way to understand me and help me speak about what has happened? I keep showing them, but they don't believe me. They just think I am being sexually aggressive (one of the staff said)."

Clearly, Marie's mother could have listened to her, but this didn't happen which is all too common. The professionals in Marie's life could have paid more attention to her behaviours and thought about the symbolism of these. They could have considered that these behaviours might be indicative of someone with a history of abuse rather than someone who is just being challenging.

Dilik

"When I was young, my parents were told that I was someone with severe Asperger's. They did not understand me and thought that having me was a punishment. I went to a boarding school near their house, but I kept running away to them. They sent me to another boarding school further away from them when I was a teenager. I didn't like it as the teachers did not understand me. I like to rock every thirty minutes for 30 seconds and that helps me stabilise. I say two sentences and then stop for a minute. I have certain clothes that I must wear, and the school forced me to put on uniform which made me itch. I am really, really interested in plastic bottles and want to collect them all. I became more and more difficult for staff to manage.

The school psychologist was asked to see me. She watched me for a week. She asked the teachers to keep a record of my 'inappropriate behaviours'. She then had a case conference with my teachers and my parents. They decided that I needed to learn more normal behaviours so that I could fit in. I was told that I needed to stop rocking and so if I didn't rock for a day, I would be given a star. I was also not allowed to have any plastic bottles. I was going to see a speech therapist who would teach me to speak three sentences at a time at least. I had to wear school uniform all the time.

I didn't like the new rules and I became worse and worse. The more I did the wrong things (their words), the stricter their rules were.

Fortunately for me, the speech therapist read a book about accommodation and helping people with Autism. She talked to the school psychologist who then asked me why rocking was important and why I only said two sentences. I said rocking helps me manage the world. The psychologist taught me to make smaller and smaller rocking movements so that I could just rock my little finger against the top of a table or desk and that was enough.

The speech therapist stopped her sessions and discussed with me why I only used two sentences. I told her that I had heard my parents say that I should only be seen and not heard. They also said that I shouldn't be allowed to say that much, perhaps two sentences at a time. This became my rule. The speech therapist helped me understand that there are many rules for speaking and that it is OK to sometimes say a lot.

I was allowed to think about plastic bottles again. They helped me buy a scrap book and put in pictures of bottles and I agreed that I could keep five real ones in my room and exchange them for another five if I wanted.

It's better here but I miss my parents a lot. Why don't they love me? What is wrong with me?"

It is a shame that we still try to fix people's differences when they have a label and yet we are all too tolerant of our own unusual habits. It is always best to ask the person to explain their behaviour rather than assume we know. A colleague once told us about a young girl with Autism who always used to run up to people and bite them. Once she had the opportunity to speak, she wanted to know why nobody liked her kisses.

Colleen

"In my family, we used to wrestle with each other a lot. It was fun and good. We shouted and made a lot of noise. The other children at nursery and big school didn't like it when I tried to do it with them at play time. I thought that it was OK for friends and family to wrestle and argue all the time like we did.

My mum helped me with keeping myself clean because it was difficult, and I was learning to make a sandwich. Mum said that, because I was twenty, I must become independent for when she went. I asked her where she would go and why I couldn't come with her. She said she would tell me later.

Mum and Dad divorced because he liked someone else, our neighbour. I heard him say once that Mum was more interested in me than him and that she shouldn't be surprised.

I went to wake Mum up one Sunday and she was not moving. My Uncle Barry, who lived with us, came back after a nightshift, and started crying. The ambulance and doctor came but they only took her away. We had the funeral and Uncle Barry and Dad said that I couldn't live with them. Social Services put me in a place a long way away from my house. I didn't know anyone, and they didn't like it when I tried to wrestle with my housemates and when I shouted and argued a lot. Then everybody started fighting with me which was good because that was how it was with my family. I carried on wrestling and arguing.

They told me that I would have to learn independent living skills. That was OK cos I wanted to live near my mum's house. But they wouldn't let me keep photos of Mum in my bedroom because I might destroy them and hurt someone if I threw them.

My social worker came and told me that I would have to move because I was too challenging for this house. What did that mean?

The new place was worse. The staff watched me all the time and I had to go to timeout if I argued or wrestled. Sometimes that was fun because they had to fight and wrestle me to go to the room."

Here we see that what is understood by professionals can be very different to what is comprehended by the person. This story also reminds us that some of our interventions, such as timeout, can have the exact opposite effect to the one we intend. The aim of timeout is to withdraw attention but the effort involved in moving the person to timeout often defeats the original purpose because so much attention is given to the person while they are being taken to timeout.

David

"I am 50 and grew up with just my dad. My mum couldn't cope with me because I am Down's. She loved me but it was too much. She left me with Dad who loves me and took my sister.

I go to a daycentre once a week and then I have a job packing shelves in the local supermarket at night. I keep forgetting things, my address and stuff.

I sometimes forget that I need to go to the toilet and wet myself. I am embarrassed and then cry a lot, even in the shop. Sometimes I can see all the people who have died in real life and TV. They stand around me and help me when I cry.

I told the manager their names and my Dad knows. He says it is OK to have pretend friends. They help me because I am lonely, and I want a girlfriend.

It is now six months later, and my Dad must have extra help for me. My friends tell me to leave the house.

The psychiatrist has told my Dad that I will get worse and then die. I heard them speaking. Why will I get worse? Somebody needs to speak to me. Who will help Dad if I die? Where will I go when I die? What is Alzheimer's?"

It is very frightening to see yourself change and not know why. We, as professionals, need to remember the important fact that our work should be *with* the person rather than *at* the person as though they were something that requires an intervention.

We can explain far more than we actually do. Our knowledge is a source of power for us, and we should be willing to let go of our facts and opinions.

Jojo

"I left my parent's place because they were getting old, and I went to live in a house with three other people. My parents were very strict and wouldn't let me go out and meet people. My mum used to go everywhere with me, even school, and she would wait in the car for an hour to make sure I was OK.

The new place was cool, they let me make my own food and I had a part-time job for a while. Then I met Will at the supermarket, and he asked me out with his mates. They showed me how to drink and smoke and have fun. Sometimes they got into trouble with police because they used to steal from the local shops. They always ran faster than me and didn't get caught. The police caught and arrested me. They told me that I had to stay out of trouble, or I would go to jail. I didn't care.

I wanted to have Will's baby so he would marry me and then we could get a house. I told him I loved him, and he called me a slag, so I slept with his mate to get him jealous.

I liked my drink a lot and the smoke. I didn't have enough money and so I used to steal from my housemates. I missed my period, and the manager took me to the doctor who said I was pregnant and must stop drinking. I didn't want to because then I wouldn't see Will at all. I kept going out without permission and meeting Will and his mates.

They got tired of me and tied me to a park bench. The police found me in the morning.

My careworker and counsellor don't know what to do with me. They are talking about a mother and baby centre but they don't know that I don't want the baby cos it isn't Will's. I am going to sneak away and buy some gin and drink it until the baby dies."

Sometimes we don't understand how lonely life can be for people who live in services and are supported by them. Equally, we don't appreciate that they can also fall victim to manipulation masked as friendliness as they may not have been able to mature as adults. Instead of helping the person think of alternative ways of living life, we sometimes (inadvertently) let them move from one dilemma to another until there is a crisis.

FURTHER QUESTIONS AND INFORMATION ON MENTAL HEALTH AND MENTAL ILLNESS (DISTRESS)

Further questions

This section contains extra questions that should only be asked by a mental health professional (clinical psychologist, counsellor or psychiatric nurse or psychiatrist). If the person themselves is going to be asked, then it is important to make sure that they feel safe during the session and have support afterwards. This should be done confidentially and discreetly.

It may be possible to answer based on prior knowledge of any history of mental health problems or illness. It is important to ask the person if they have a history of mental illness (distress) even if they have not previously declared one.

More information is available from:

www.nimh.nih.gov,
www.nhs.uk/conditions/stress-anxiety-depression,
www.mind.org.uk,
American Psychological Association Help Center.

In the last month…

1.   How many symptoms of anxiety and worry did the person show (worry, difficulty breathing etc.)?

☐   1

☐   5

☐   10

☐   Many

Anxiety symptoms include worry and physical reactions such as increased blood pressure, tension, problems breathing sweating, trembling. People with anxiety disorders can have recurring intrusive thoughts or concerns. They may avoid certain situations because of worry.

Worry involves excess concern about something that could happen.

2. How many symptoms of depression did the person show (sadness, feeling tired all the time)?

☐ None

☐ One or two

☐ Five

☐ Ten

☐ Twenty plus

Depression is more than just sadness. People with depression may show limited interest and pleasure in daily life, gain, or lose weight, have insomnia, or sleep too much, lack energy and motivation, find it difficult to remember or concentrate or pay attention, feel very unworthy and sometimes feel suicidal.

3. How fearful was the person?

☐ No fears

☐ Reasonable amount of fear demonstrated

☐ Demonstrated significant fears (phobias) that substantially interfere with life

Fear is a part of our lives and generally we cope with its presence in healthy ways. Sometimes, however, it can become excessive and a phobia. These can have a negative impact on the person, e.g. avoiding stimuli that trigger the fear.

4. What signs were there of any intention to commit suicide?

☐ None

☐ One negative comment, e.g. 'What's the point?'

☐ More than two

☐ Used the word 'suicide' or other negative comments a lot

☐ Evidence that there was a concrete plan

Examples of behaviours of concern include negative utterances, e.g. 'What is the point? 'I will end it all'. There could be evidence of plans to accompany thoughts and words, e.g. collecting medication, very high levels of anxiety and/or depression and/or paranoia and/ substance misuse.

The person may have very limited life problem solving approaches and many psychosocial stressors may be present as well as a history of trauma and previous attempts.

5. How many obsessive-compulsive behaviours did the person have (intrusive thoughts, compulsive behaviours, e.g. cleaning, hoarding)?

☐ None

☐ Ordinary thoughts and/or behaviours

☐ Behaviours and/or thoughts that interfered significantly with life

Obsessive Compulsive Behaviours (Obsessive Compulsive Disorder, OCD). This consists of recurrent intrusive thoughts (obsessions) which can lead to rituals (compulsions), sometimes to reduce the occurrence of the thoughts. They are often acknowledged by individuals with OCD, are time consuming, lead to distress and negatively impact daily life.

6. How ordinary were their eating habits (within the normal range or over-eating or undereating)?

☐ Within the expected range

☐ Abnormal (eating too little)

☐ Abnormal (eating too much)

7. How much alcohol did the person consume?

☐ None

☐ Equivalent of two glasses per day

☐ More than one bottle of wine/day

Average consumption is expected to be one glass a day for women and two for men, e.g. a glass of beer or wine (Mayo Clinic).

8. How many cigarettes (including vaping) did the person use per day?

☐ None

☐ Five

☐ More than ten

9. To what extent did the person misuse other substances, e.g. prescription medication, illegal substances?

☐ None

☐ Once a week

☐ More than once a week

(If there has been use, what are the legal implications?)

10. How oriented was the person in reality, e.g. aware of date and time?

☐ Completely oriented

☐ Some disorientation

☐ Very disoriented

11. What was the history of any head injuries? What were the prognoses? What is the current impact on the person?

12. What, if any, cognitive problems were indicated, e.g. memory and/or expressive language problems, e.g. very forgetful?

☐ None

☐ A few examples

☐ Many daily examples

13. To what extent was the person paranoid?

☐ No evidence

☐ A few examples

☐ Ample evidence

Paranoia occurs when the person becomes extremely suspicious about someone or something. It is not rational and can lead to upsetting thinking and behaviours.

14. What was the evidence that the person experienced flashbacks (recurring memories of past events)?

☐ None

☐ One per week

☐ At least one per day

Flashbacks can occur for a variety of reasons and are not always indicative of Post Traumatic Stress Disorder. They can be visual or auditory or through physical sensation. They may lead to the person being dissociated from reality at least for a short period. The person often feels disoriented afterwards.

15. How many hallucinations did the person have?

☐ None

☐ One a week

☐ One a day

☐ All the time

Hallucinations: the person experiences something (visual, auditory, or sensory) that does not exist in reality. They often experience and act as though it is real. Causes vary from substance misuse to mental distress. It is important to explore the hallucination and not dispute its existence, unless in therapy. Extra efforts may be needed to help the person be and feel safe.

16. How many delusions did they have?

☐ None

☐ One a week

☐ One a day

☐ All the time

A person's delusion can be a very complex belief system which they hold onto despite contradictory evidence and reason.

17. How social was the person?

☐ Gregarious

☐ Liked to socialise appropriately

☐ Preferred own company

☐ Anti-social

18. How narcissistic was the person (only thinks of themselves)?

☐ Considerate

☐ Thought of others some of the time

☐ Thought of others only a little

☐ Put themselves first all the time

19. How energetic was the person?

☐ Low energy levels

☐ Average energy levels

☐ Very high levels of energy

If the person has low amounts of energy, then they could be depressed; very high levels could indicate manic behaviour or ADHD.

Information on mental health and mental illness (distress)

Phobias

A phobia is an anxiety disorder, which is characterised by an irrational, extreme fear related to a specific trigger—this may be a person, event, situation, place, object, or animal. A phobia differs from a fear, in part, because of the consistently excessive nature of the reaction, that is not ameliorated by information, support or encouragement.

People can learn to manage their reactions to the triggers or the phobia in general, partly through therapy and/or medication.

www.nhs.uk/conditions/phobias/

Anxiety

It's normal to feel anxious occasionally, and it often occurs because of stress or threat. High levels of consistent anxiety can have very adverse effects on a person.

There are several types of anxiety disorders. All are characterised by persistent or severe fear, in situations where most people wouldn't feel threatened.

Cognitive behavioural and other therapies can help the individual manage their anxieties so that they can live full lives.

https://www.nimh.nih.gov/health/topics/anxiety-disorders/index.shtml

Depression

The National Institute for Mental Health (United States) (www.nimh.nih.gov) notes that "major depressive disorder or clinical depression is a common but serious mood disorder". Symptoms can include: a persistent sad, anxious, or 'empty' mood; feelings of hopelessness or pessimism; irritability; feelings of guilt; worthlessness or helplessness; loss of interest or pleasure in activities; decreased appetite; fatigue; restlessness; difficulty concentrating, poor memory, indecision; changes in sleeping patterns and eating habits; reckless behaviour; unexplained physical pain, such as backache or headache; and thoughts of death or suicide.

People can be helped to live with depression. A combination of therapy (usually Cognitive Behavioural), medication and self-help can be effective.

https://www.nimh.nih.gov/health/topics/depression/index.shtml

Schizophrenia

The National Institute of Mental Health in the United States (www.nimh.nih.gov) describes schizophrenia as a chronic and severe mental illness (distress)/disorder which affects a person's thoughts, feelings, and behaviour. People with schizophrenia are sometimes described as having an entirely distinct interpretation of reality, and real events than others, and their interpretation is often very vivid and alarming to them.

The symptoms can be very disabling, disrupting a person's ability to function in their work, relationships, and household. The thoughts and feelings associated with schizophrenia can be highly distressing and frustrating, both to the individual and to those who know and care for them.

However, while living with schizophrenia may not always be easy, it is possible to have a reasonable life including work and managing relapses.

http://www.nimh.nih.gov/health/topics/schizophrenia/index.shtml

Obsessive Compulsive Disorder

Obsessive-Compulsive Disorder (OCD) is a severe anxiety disorder, characterised by frequent intrusive and unwelcome obsessional thoughts and often associated behaviours. Some studies indicate that there is a genetic component to this disorder, although OCD behaviours may also be learned and based on habits developed over a long period.

With help, people with OCD can learn how to handle everyday life and their obsession and/or compulsion.

https://www.ocduk.org/

Stress

Stress is our body's response to things that we consider threatening to our peace of mind and safety. We often refer to our *fight-or-flight* response, which kicks in when we sense danger. When we feel threatened, our nervous system releases hormones, including adrenaline (which increases our capacity to focus and act) and cortisol (a stress-relieving hormone)—these ready us to face a challenge and act. However, these can also lead to us feeling confused and unable to make decisions as well as tending to resort to our biases and preferences instead of treating the situation as brand new. We can learn more about our stress reactions and how to cope.

www.nhs.uk/conditions/stress-anxiety-depression/understanding-stress/

Sleep

Sleep allows our bodies and minds to recover, repair and rejuvenate from the stresses of our daily lives. It is vital for our health and wellbeing. Research indicates that we need, on average, eight hours of sleep per day. Older adults still need eight hours per day but may find it difficult to have that amount of sleep. Children are likely to need more.

Sufficient sleep means that our cognitive (memory, thinking, decision-making and language) functions can be more effective. Similarly, creativity, productivity and emotional stability are enhanced as well as concentration.

Sleep problems can be addressed by first understanding the current pattern, investigating reasons, and then making necessary changes. This is known as sleep hygiene.

The psychology of pain

Pain is more than a physical sensation—it has psychological, emotional, and biological components. These influence the intensity with which individuals experience pain, how debilitating the pain is, and if treatment is likely to be effective. The typical emotional reaction to pain includes anxiety, fear, anger, guilt, frustration, and depression. Emotions shape our experience of the pain via neural connections and are powerful drivers of behaviour. We can learn to manage our pain.

Psychological resilience

All of us experience change, challenges, unexpected and traumatic events in our lives. How well we respond to and cope with this is described as resilience. Some people can survive incredibly difficult situations and experiences in their lives, be apparently emotionally intact, but struggle with things which others might consider everyday obstacles. Some people are very vulnerable to any change and need additional support to process and manage these things. There are programmes available to help people learn about becoming more resilient using positive psychology.

Addictions/Substance Misuse

When a person is addicted to something, they are unable to voluntarily control how they use it and become dependent on it to cope with daily life. Addiction may refer to a substance dependence (e.g. illicit or prescription drugs, nicotine or alcohol) or behavioural addiction (e.g. gambling or shopping). It is a compulsive behaviour and interferes with the person's ability to manage life responsibilities such as work and relationships and may impact negatively on their health.

People can get help from a variety of sources: residential facilities, community programmes, groups such as Al-Anon.

Cognitive Behavioural Therapy

Cognitive Behavioural Therapy (CBT) focuses on supporting an individual to recognise their own patterns of behaviour and thought processes (cognitive), and develop strategies to retrain and manage them and change the way they react and behave (behavioural). The therapist works with the individual to break down problems that seem overwhelming into smaller parts and then devise practical ways of managing or resolving those problems.

CBT is commonly used to treat anxiety and depression and other mental health problems such as OCD, phobias, eating problems, etc.

The psychology of motivation

Motivation is a driver for change or action. It can be described as a desire or need for an outcome that provokes action. The strength of that feeling or desire enables us to focus on, plan and continue to work towards that envisaged outcome. Motivation is usually dependent on a perceived goal. Motivation is underpinned by the emotional, social, financial, physical, and cognitive reasons for focusing on that goal.

It is important to understand our levels of motivation and how we use it. Then, we can be more effective in our lives.

Will power and self-discipline

'Will power' and 'self-discipline' are terms we often associate with physical health and wellbeing, in the context of diet and exercise; we make conscious decisions to regulate ourselves and our actions.

To do this, we must confront our instincts and impulses with better judgement and resolve, override our desires and impulses, and give up short-term gratification with a view to long-term benefits.

Wellbeing

Wellbeing broadly refers to our sense that our life is going well, considering both our mental health and physical health. We assess our wellbeing based on our environment, our emotions, our assessment of ourselves in relation to others, and our perceptions of how others perceive us. We can learn more about enhancing our wellbeing.

http://www.cdc.gov/hrqol/wellbeing.htm

Healthy living

A great many factors affect our health. Some of these are beyond our control, such as our genetic makeup or our age. But we can make changes to our lifestyles to help reduce our risk of certain diseases, including heart disease, cancer, and diabetes.

Eating well and taking regular exercise can have a substantial and positive effect on our mental health and are essential components of feeling well and calm.

www.nhs.uk/livewell/healthy-eating/pages/healthyeating.aspx

Effective work relationships

Good work relationships are important and can lead to better job satisfaction, increased productivity as well as personal growth. This can be achieved by being consistent, honest, trustworthy, and supportive. It is important not to engage in gossip and other negative activities.

Happiness

Most of us would agree that we want to find happiness in life. But we often fail to recognise and take the proactive steps that would help us to achieve it. Over the past 15 years, a considerable amount of psychological research has been undertaken to better understand how we might take control of our own happiness. Studies have identified several effective strategies, including:

appreciating and being grateful for what we have,

finding meaning and purpose in our lives and our work,

forging strong social bonds,

acting altruistically,

relaxing our desire to maximise our benefit,

letting go.

These behaviours have been shown to enhance happiness and satisfaction during good times, and build the resilience needed during tough times. We can learn more about happiness and resilience and see what could change in our lives.

QUESTIONS AND INFORMATION ON LEARNING DISABILITIES/ DIFFICULTIES

If the person you are working to help has been assessed as a person with learning disabilities or difficulties, then it can be important to know more about their symptoms and signs as they can impact on their life and the support they may need. However, it is important to remember that, for about half of the people with such differences, the exact reasons are unknown. It is therefore important to conduct a thorough assessment. The instrument of choice is often the WAIS (Wechsler Adult Intelligence Scale IV) which is also available in different languages. Although a problem with the WAIS is that performance can be dependent on the amount of traditional schooling a person has had and their ability to respond in timed tests. An alternative global assessment is Ravens Progressive Matrices as this is non-verbal and not timed.

While such assessments can be useful, it is also vital to look at how the person is living their life, their coping skills in daily living etc. This can involve an assessment of activities of daily living.

Generalised learning difficulties

A person who is said to have generalised learning difficulties can have problems with understanding, communicating, memory, concentration, and attention. They could also have speech problems, find it difficult to take care of themselves in terms of personal hygiene or moving around in the community, etc.

Once the nature of their talents and difficulties is known, then the person can be helped to live a good life in their community in a way that suits them. Sometimes, they may need extra support, e.g. to shop. Care needs to be taken that they are not lonely and/or only surrounded by paid professionals and that they are doing what they want and in which they are interested.

Attention-Deficit/Hyperactivity Disorder (ADHD)

The National Institute of Mental Health (NIHM) in the United States describes ADHD as an "ongoing pattern of inattention and/or hyperactivity-impulsivity that interferes with functioning or development of the person."

Inattention—the person finds it difficult to concentrate and can be disorganised.

Hyperactivity—they are very active and find it difficult to sit still for long periods. The person may have developed their own self-management strategies.

Impulsivity—they can act without stopping to think or reflect when making decisions. They may be socially inappropriate such as constantly interrupting.

These difficulties can significantly interfere with a person's capacity to function in life. A thorough assessment is needed to better understand what issues the person may face. Once this has been done, there are many therapeutic interventions that can be used to help, e.g. teaching the person self-control and/or distraction techniques, showing them how to relax and cope differently. Medication can help but needs to be prescribed and monitored by a specialist doctor, e.g. a neurologist or psychiatrist.

Down's Syndrome

Down's Syndrome is a chromosomal condition. People with Down's Syndrome are likely to demonstrate key traits which include low muscle tone, small stature, an upward slant to their eyes, a deep crease in their palms and some intellectual difficulties. People with Down's can live full lives in their communities, sometimes with support. Unfortunately, they can be more prone to developing dementia at an earlier age than other populations.

http://www.ndss.org/

Autism

People with Autism or Asperger's tend to have a range of characteristics. Each person will be different in their skills, talents, and difficulties. The typical person with Autism or Asperger's does not exist. It is therefore very important to take time to understand each person, who they are, how they live and how they cope, as well as how they interact with others.

Formally, the Diagnostic and Statistical Manual of Mental Disorders 5 includes Asperger's Syndrome under the category of Autism (Autism Spectrum Disorder (ASD)). This has led to some controversy and concern, not least from people with Asperger's themselves. Pervasive developmental disorders (not otherwise specified) is also included.

People with Autism or Asperger's can show certain characteristics, in varying degrees, such as:

difficulties in understanding social interactions and empathy,
specific ways of communicating verbally and non-verbally,
repetitive patterns of behaviour such as hand flapping.

Sometimes, the person does not like change and prefers a set daily routine.

Some people may have a topic in which they are extremely interested. This can remain the same for years or could change, e.g. a life-long interest in tropical plants versus becoming interested in one film and then, six months later, switching to another film. These are known as focused interests.

The first step is to understand what characteristics the person has, and if any of them are negatively impacting on how they are living. People with Asperger's and Autism can also learn about social interactions by being taught as they sometimes don't, as easily, learn the subtle lessons of life such as how to make and keep friends, that taste exists, etc.

www.autism.org.uk/

Rett Syndrome

Rett Syndrome is a neurodevelopmental disorder much more common in females than males. People with Rett's have numerous difficulties, e.g. eating, speaking, breathing easily. These can increase as the person gets older.

If a person has been assessed as someone with Rett's, then it is important to learn as much as possible about this and then help family and friends adjust their expectations about the person who is still a full human being but is likely to live a different life to that which was initially expected.

https://www.rettsyndrome.org/

Lesch-Nyhan Syndrome

Lesch-Nyhan Syndrome is a rare, inherited disorder that affects boys at a very young age. It impairs how the body builds and breaks down purines. Symptoms include joint swelling, neuro-difficulties, and behavioural problems.

Again, it is absolutely vital to have a proper assessment and learn as much as possible about the person and their characteristics. They are likely to self-injure and so the expectation should not be to hope that this will stop and disappear but on how to help the person be safer and more appropriate and safer in their actions.

http://www.lesch-nyhan.org/en

Prader-Willi Syndrome

Prader-Willi Syndrome (PWS) is a rare genetic condition, found in both males and females, which affects appetite, growth, cognitive function, and behaviour. People with Prader-Willi can have problems with managing their eating and may not mature sexually. They can and do live full lives in their societies. Support can be given to help them manage their appetites as well as consider how they will cope and live in society in a way that respects them for who they are and want to be.

http://www.pwsausa.org

QUESTIONS AND CONCEPTS TO HELP WITH SYSTEMS THINKING

Some of these may be helpful as you work to aid the person by giving you a greater understanding of organisational perspectives and issues.

Questions

Please remember to be selective and choose only the most important questions. We can always ask a hundred questions but doing so may blur our thinking. Some of these questions will need to be asked sensitively and in a respectful manner. It is worth thinking who will ask and what is needed to help people respond to these questions.

1. How inclusive is the organisation towards people with distress factors and reactions? (Place a mark on the line to represent where each group is).

Senior leadership

Very inclusive--- Exclude

Professionals (Health and Social Care)

Very inclusive--- Exclude

Managers

Very inclusive--- Exclude

Staff

Very inclusive--- Exclude

2. What is the skill set for supporting people with distress factors and reactions? Please complete the table below.

Group	Very limited proficiency and understanding	Some skills	Experts
Senior leadership			
Managers			
Professionals (Health and Social Care)			
Family and friends			
Support and care staff			

3. What is the level of willingness, motivation, and drive for change to better support the person? Place a mark on the continuum to indicate position in terms of willingness etc.

Senior leadership

None at all------------------------- Some ------------------------Total commitment

Managers

None at all------------------------- Some ------------------------Total commitment

Professionals (Health and Social Care)

None at all------------------------- Some ------------------------Total commitment

Support and care staff

None at all------------------------- Some ------------------------Total commitment

Family

None at all------------------------- Some ------------------------Total commitment

Informal supporters

None at all------------------------- Some ------------------------Total commitment

4. What resources have been made or are likely to be made available? Place a mark on the line to reflect the current situation.

As much as is required --------------------Some --------------------------------None

Information

The psychology of respect

Respect is an important component of self-identity and relationships. It tends to be a self-reinforcing behaviour—if you treat others with respect, you're more likely to be treated with respect in turn.

Treating someone with respect means that you demonstrate the same for that person and acknowledge all their qualities. You value their feelings and opinions even if they are different to yours. The person is considered as an equal to you and others.

Thinking about respect when you are helping someone with their distress factors and reactions can lead to different outcomes. It can also help when you are looking at who will support them and how this can be done with respect.

Holloman, H. & Yates, P. H. (2013) Cloudy with a chance of sarcasm or sunny with high expectations: using best practice language to strengthen positive behaviour intervention and support efforts. *Journal of Positive Behaviour Interventions*, 15 (2) 124–127.

Price-Mitchell, M. (2014) *The Language of Respect: Walking our talk with teenagers.* Published online at: https://www.psychologytoday.com/us/blog/the-momentyouth/201402/the-language-respect

Collaboration in teams and organisations

Collaboration in the workplace is about bringing people together to pool their ideas, perspectives, skills, experience, and capacity to accomplish a common goal. It relies on a strong sense of shared purpose. Team members need to recognise and embrace the value in working together, as a way of achieving tasks and goals more effectively and efficiently than they could if working alone.

Effective collaboration enables managers and organisations to draw together the diverse skills and strengths of different individuals, to create a team that is far more effective than a group of individuals working alone.

Gratton, L. and Erickson, T. J. (2007) Eight ways to build collaborative teams. *Harvard Business Review*, November. Available online at: https://hbr.org/2007/11/ eight-way s-to-build-collaborative-teams

Understanding and managing cultural differences

Mental ill health does not recognise cultural boundaries. However, people's culture—be it family culture, national culture, religious culture, work culture—gives a vital context to how some people's problems have developed, and how they might be supported to get well. In addition to this, we all work in multicultural teams to some extent—even if that multiculturalism only refers to people's differing social or regional backgrounds. It is a helpful way of focusing on people's individuality and trying to approach their difficulties from their perspective, rather than from our own.

Fons Trompenaars built on the work of Geert Hofstede and identified through research, seven qualities with which to consider cultures: universalism–particularism, individualism–communitarianism, specific–diffuse, neutral–emotional, achievement–ascription, sequential time–synchronous time, internal direction–outer direction. Erin Meyer has used their concepts and describes them in a practical manner.

Trompenaars, F. and Hampden-Turner, C. (1997) *Riding the Waves of Culture: Understanding cultural diversity in business.* London: Nicholas Brealey Publishing Ltd.

Meyer, E. (2015) *The Culture Map.* Pennsylvania, US: Ingram Publishing Services.

Problem Solving

Creative Problem Solving (CPS) is an innovative method of approaching problems or challenges and trying to find positive, and creative solutions. The method involves breaking down a problem into smaller parts as a way of better understanding it, then generating ideas to address and solve the problem. From there you, and others possibly, collaborate to evaluate those ideas and find the most effective solutions.

The approach was originated by Alex Osborn in the 1940s, and further developed by Osborn and Sidney Parnes. Their Creative Problem Solving Process (CPSP) has been taught at the International Centre for Studies in Creativity at Buffalo College in Buffalo, New York since the 1950s (http://creativeproblemsolving.com/).

The shadow side of organisations

Carl Jung theorised that we all have a shadow side to our personality, an unacknowledged, unconscious side, driven by emotions such as fear, anxiety, jealousy, greed, and spite. We try to repress and ignore this shadow side, but it is there in every individual. Jung argues that to know ourselves and make the most of our potential, we need to recognise, accept, and manage the dark aspects of our personalities.

Several psychologists have applied Jung's theory of the shadow side to the organisational context. Organisations are, after all, collections of individual people, with all of their strengths, talents, complexities and flaws. Within the workplace, the shadow side exists at both an individual and an organisational level.

What are the golden and shadow sides of the organisations that support the person with distress factors and reactions?

How will these help or hinder the interventions to help the person? What needs to be done differently to address these concerns?

Crisis management

Much has been written about crisis management and little is traditionally applied in human services at the level of the person for whom the services exist. The two main types of crises are managed and unmanaged crises (Lagadec). The response to crises can be biased even if there are effective plans in place. For example, there is a tendency to decide the nature of the crisis quite early on and stop paying attention to information that comes in at a later stage. A good crisis management system will not only have carried out risk assessments, but will also have thorough plans for mitigation, and be responsive etc.

Furthermore, those responsible for dealing with a crisis should have been trained and participated in rehearsals. These will enable responders to internally record memories of actions to take, should an incident occur, if they remember to remain flexible in the situation as it will not be the same as the rehearsal.

https://www.youtube.com/watch?v=xM1c6HM7u3k

Risk management

Much of the work will involve the daily assessment and management of different types of risk to clients and services. Many factors feed into this critical aspect of caring for those with distress factors and reactions—one of the major factors in risk management is prioritization of identified risks and how to address them, within the realities of workload, resource, and budget considerations. Having identified risks and a way forward, co-ordination is often a critical aspect of minimizing and monitoring risk going forward.

Risks may include a wide range of internal or external factors that could impact on the viability of care provision, a project or organisation—from cost increases and funding cuts to political and organisational change, and traumatic events. Strategies to manage threats include "avoiding the threat or reducing the negative effect or probability of the threat, transferring all or part of the threat to another party", or finding ways to benefit from the potential or actual consequences of a particular threat.

Risk management should be a structured, integral part of organisational processes, informing decision-making and planning. It also needs to be dynamic and responsive to change. The process should create value for the organization so that the resources used for mitigation are not greater than doing nothing.

https://en.wikipedia.org/wiki/Risk_management

Collective leadership

'Collective leadership is leadership that prioritises leadership of all, by all and together with all.'

Michael West, 2014

Traditional leadership is often seen as a function located in one person with the necessary authority to fulfil that role. However, this function is meaningless without others. Collective leadership is seen as a process that involves many people with clear roles and functions to operationalise the vision and associated objectives.

What is the quality of leadership in those providing services to the person with distress factors and reactions? How could this become more collective, collaborative, and supportive?

West, M. (2014) *Collective Leadership: Fundamental to creating the cultures we need in the NHS.* London: King's Fund.

www.ingramcontent.com/pod-product-compliance
Lightning Source LLC
Chambersburg PA
CBHW042353030426
42336CB00029B/3468